THE COMPLETE RESOURCE BOOK FOR INFANTS

Dedication

To Baby Evan and Baby Quinn—may your journeys be filled with wonder!

Additional books written by Pam Schiller

Creating Readers: Over 1000 Games, Activities, Tongue Twisters, Fingerplays, Songs, and Stories to Get Children Excited About Reading

The Complete Resource Book: An Early Childhood Curriculum, with Kay Hastings

The Complete Book of Rhymes, Songs, Poems, Fingerplays, and Chants, with Jackie Silberg

The Complete Book of Activities, Games, Stories, Props, Recipes, and Dances, with Jackie Silberg

Start Smart! Building Brain Power in the Early Years

The Practical Guide to Quality Child Care, with Patricia Carter Dyke

The Values Book, with Tamera Bryant

Count on Math, with Lynne Peterson

Where Is Thumbkin?, with Thomas Moore

Instant Curriculum, with Joan Rosanno

Do You Know the Muffin Man? with Thomas Moore

A Pam Schiller Book

The Complete Resource Book for Infants

Over 700 Experiences for Children from Birth to 18 Months

Pam Schiller

Photographs by Mary Duru

Illustrations by Deborah Wright

gryphon house
Lewisville, NC

© 2005 Pam Schiller
Printed in the United States of America.

Published by Gryphon House, Inc.
PO Box 10, Lewisville, NC 27023
800.638.0928 (toll-free); 877.638.7576 (fax)

Visit us on the web at www.gryphonhouse.com

Reprinted June 2014

Library of Congress Cataloging-in-Publication Data

Schiller, Pamela Byrne.
  The complete resource book for infants : experiences for children from birth to 18 months / Pam Schiller ; illustrations by Deborah Wright.
       p. cm.
  Summary: "Resource book for teachers of children ages birth to 18 months, including information on creating an appropriate environment, and activities to use in the classroom"--Provided by publisher.
  Includes bibliographical references and index.
  ISBN: 978-0-87659-295-3
  1. Infants. I. Title.
  HQ774.S333 2005

                             2005003164

Bulk purchase
Gryphon House books are available for special premiums and sales promotions as well as for fund-raising use. Special editions or book excerpts also can be created to specification. For details, contact the Director of Marketing at Gryphon House.

Disclaimer
Gryphon House, Inc. and the author cannot be held responsible for damage, mishap, or injury incurred during the use of or because of activities in this book. Appropriate and reasonable caution and adult supervision of children involved in activities and corresponding to the age and capability of each child involved, is recommended at all times. Do not leave children unattended at any time. Observe safety and caution at all times.

Every effort has been made to locate copyright and permission information.

Table of Contents

Chapter 2
Social/Emotional Development—Becoming a Social Being

Chapter 3
Physical Development—
Moving and Exploring

Chapter 4
Cognitive Development—
Making Sense of the World

Appendix

Index

Introduction

Preparing the Infant Learning Environment

There is a high level of agreement among experts about the primary characteristics of a quality infant learning environment:

- The classroom must be safe.
- The caregiver must be warm, loving, responsive, and permanent.
- Communication between families and caregivers must be a priority.
  (Baker and Manfredi-Pettit, 2004)

The Classroom Must Be Safe

The learning environment includes everything that is inside and outside the classroom. Here are some suggestions for maintaining a safe environment.

*"What I learn from birth to three is what will matter most to me." **

1. Keep your attention on the children at all times. It is easy to become distracted as family members come and go, when one child demands attention, when preparing a bottle, and during other daily responsibilities; however, keeping your eye on all the children is essential to ensure their safety at all times.
2. Check toys daily to make sure that they are in good working condition. Watch for sharp edges and loose parts. Remove any that are unsafe and/or need to be repaired.
3. Keep electrical outlets covered.
4. Install latches on low cabinets and drawers.
5. Store toys in open containers. Avoid toy chests with lids because a child could become trapped inside.
6. Provide toys that can be washed easily.
7. Wash toys throughout the day. Babies put everything in their mouths.
8. Use a Small Object Tester (available from most school supply companies) to determine that toys are large enough that they cannot be swallowed. Remove any objects that are too small.

*This slogan is copyrighted. It comes printed on several items from Noodle Soup, a direct-mail business in Cleveland, Ohio. Call 800-795-9295 for a free copy of their catalog or check their website at www.noodlesoup.com.

9. Check equipment once a week to identify items that may need repair, such as cribs with loose sides, feeding tables with loose straps, and so on. Check outdoor equipment for sharp edges and splintered wood. Repair or remove any equipment that needs it.

10. Provide plenty of space for crawling, creeping, and toddling. Avoid using walkers and carriers.

11. Keep diaper pails, trashcans, and other inappropriate items out of the reach of children.

12. Check the sides of cribs and trays of feeding tables to be sure they are locked in place at all times.

The Caregiver Must Be Warm, Loving, Responsive, and Permanent

As a caregiver, you are a core component of the infant environment. You are responsible for understanding children's stages of development; communicating with children, families, and other staff; and creating experiences and activities that maximize opportunities for children's optimum growth and development.

Infants are at the most dramatic and dynamic stage of development of their lives: mentally, physically, socially, and emotionally. An infant caregiver plays a major role in each child's development. Knowing what is appropriate at each stage of development, staying informed with the latest information from early brain development research, and watching for cues from infants that indicate where they might be on the growth and development continuum are the basics that determine your interactions with each child.

Communication Between Families and Caregivers Must Be a Priority

Good communication is vital to your relationship with both infants and their families. Each infant needs to know that you are the primary source of support when family members are away. Your interactions with infants and your attention to their needs will help them learn this. Families, too, must be able to trust that you are standing in for them while they are away from their child. You will gain this special trust as they watch your relationship with their baby develop.

In addition, it is essential to communicate effectively with fellow staff members. Good communication enables the classroom routines and transitions to run smoothly. Transferring information effectively between yourself and other staff members, between yourself and families, and between yourself and the children will prevent turmoil later.

What Constitutes Infant Curriculum?

With older children, daily lessons focus on conceptual themes and are prepared around the structure of circle time activities and learning centers. Skills are integrated into instruction to provide intentionality (educational purpose). In infant classrooms, daily experiences focus on developmental domains or on the practice of a specific skill (infant accomplishments) and are prepared around spontaneous activities that are likely to occur in the context of daily care and routines.

The developmental domains that are the essential building blocks for infants are language, cognitive, social/emotional, and motor development. Many aspects of development occur in more than one domain. For example, cause and effect is a primary goal of both cognitive and social development during the first year of life. Although cause and effect is a cognitive and social/emotional goal, it will develop with experiences in all areas of development. For example, a baby's understanding of the *I coo, you listen, and then I coo again* interchange that happens as language develops is a cause-and-effect experience. Pushing the buttons on a busy box is a motor experience, but the outcome will be both the development of coordination and the understanding of cause and effect. Peek-a-boo is a social activity, but playing it reinforces cause-and-effect relationships. The reactions that baby gets from the caregiver when she looks for a hidden toy will support her cognitive development and reinforce the concept of cause and effect. In the infant classroom, the acquisition of skills is an integrated process.

Cause and effect is one goal for infants, but there are many others. Exploration, perception, communication, mobility, self-competence, trust, relationships, independence, and impulse control (around 18 months) are all goals of development for infants. Experiences and activities that support these areas make the best "curriculum" for infants. Each area of development and the related "themes" are explained in the introduction sections of each chapter. A developmental checklist can be found on pages 250–252 in the appendix.

Early Brain Development Research

The first three years of life lay the foundation for lifelong learning. The child's brain is busy wiring itself to develop vision, emotional stability, language development, motor development, thinking skills, and much more (Shore, 1997). Thanks to the new imaging technology used in neurobiology, scientists can now look inside the brains of living children and adults to see the brain in action—how it grows, how it acts, and how it reacts. It is possible to determine when specific areas of the brain are wired and how that wiring can be reinforced for positive outcomes. This information provides the optimum opportunity to give children a healthy and strong foundation for lifelong learning (Shore, 1997; Ramey and Ramey, 1999).

Windows of Opportunity

Critical windows of opportunity (fertile times) for wiring the brain exist that should not be missed during these early years. These windows provide a timetable for when experiences are particularly important or when some skills are more readily learned.

The brain is the only unfinished organ at birth. Babies are born with 100 billion nerve cells, called neurons. Only a small number of these neurons are connected at birth. Through experiences and interactions with others, the infant's brain will forge an estimated 1,000 trillion synapses (connections). The synapses form pathways between neurological communities. Neural pathways that are used become stronger. Those that are not used will eventually fade away. Experience wires the brain. Repetition of experiences strengthens the wiring. The windows of opportunity provide the timetable for when specific kinds of experiences are most likely to wire and strengthen specific skills. The chart below shows the windows of opportunity and the timetable for wiring and enhancement of wiring. The only window that slams shut is the window for visual wiring. If babies don't have appropriate visual experiences during the first two years of life they will not be wired appropriately for vision.

The brain has a high level of plasticity during the first 10 to 12 years of life, and during this time wiring and rewiring are regular occurrences. However, when something is wired and that wiring is reinforced with repeated experiences it becomes more difficult to change (Shore, 1997; Ramey and Ramey, 1999; Brazelton, 1992; Nash, 1997).

Window for:	Wiring Window	Greatest Enhancement Opportunity
Language	4–8 months	8 months–6 years
Early Sounds	4–8 months	8 months–6 years
Vocabulary Development	Birth–24 months	2–7 years
Emotional Intelligence	Birth–48 months	4–8 years
Trust	Birth–14 months	4–8 years
Impulse Control	15 months–48 months	4–8 years
Social Attachment	Birth–24 months	2–5 years
Motor Development	Birth–24 months	2–5 years
Thinking Skills	Birth–48 months	4 years–puberty
Cause and Effect	Birth–15 months	15 months–puberty
Problem Solving	15 months–48 months	18 months–puberty
Vision	Birth–24 months	2–6 years
Second Language	Birth–60 months	6 years–puberty

Responding to Infant Cues

Babies are good at providing cues that inform us of their readiness to play, eat, sleep, retreat, and much more. Babies communicate with both verbal and nonverbal cues. Cues vary from child to child. A skilled caregiver becomes familiar with each child's unique style of communication and, by using these cues, is able to respond quickly and accurately to babies' needs. The list below describes a variety of cues babies may provide in an attempt to communicate their needs.

Signal	Verbal Cues	Nonverbal Cues
Ready for activity	giggling babbling smiling laughing talking feeding sounds	eyes widening facial brightening hands open head raising
Needs a rest (break)	whimpering whining crying fussing spitting	breaking eye contact clinching eyes frowning lowering brow hiccupping pouting face yawning joined hands hands to ears hands behind head/back of neck hands to mouth hands to stomach increased feet movement leg kicking straightening arms and/or legs stiffening body lowering head back arch turning head away pulling away

		pushing away
		shaking head "no"
		crawling away
		walking away
		vomiting
Hungry	whining crying fussing	sucking hands to mouth chewing hands clinging tray pounding
Sleepy	whining fussing crying	rubbing eyes lowering eyes turning head away pulling away yawning rocking

Using Sign Language as a Means of Communicating

Frustration related to an inability to communicate accounts for many of the emotional meltdowns infants and toddlers experience. Infants between the ages of 9 and 18 months are capable of understanding far more than they are able to communicate. They are also capable of developing ideas and thoughts but are unable yet to verbally express those ideas and thoughts to the adults around them. Providing an alternative means of communication can make this period of time less stressful for both children and the adults around them.

Baby sign language is currently being used successfully in both home and schools across the country. Shaking the head or moving the hands is far easier to learn than the intricate manipulation of the lips, jaw, and tongue necessary for each new word. Large muscle coordination is learned before small muscle coordination—at about the same time children want to express themselves.

A number of books offer simple signs that are easily taught to infants, but you can create your own signs. It is important to remember that signs need to be simple and natural. If you decide to make up your own signs, share them with families so that they can use and reinforce the same signs at home. The important signs for children include those that pertain to their needs—I'm hungry, I'm thirsty, change me, pick me up, put me down—and those that help them express their wishes—all done, more, and let's go.

Simple signs (see pages 247–249) not only assist in correctly interpreting children's needs and desires, but also they help with transitions. They will help you connect with children in a richer and much more significant way. You will find you have fewer conflicts, less grabbing, fewer temper tantrums, and a lot more peace in the classroom.

Developmental Expectations and Assessment

Knowing what to expect of babies as they grow and develop is critical to providing appropriate activities, recognizing signs of trouble, and communicating accurately with families. Infants are diverse in their developmental capabilities. This diversity reinforces the concept that each child's journey is individual and unique. However, there are developmental norms that provide a guide. An awareness of the norms is crucial to guiding children on their developmental journey.

Knowing what to expect of babies as they grow and develop is critical to providing appropriate activities, recognizing signs of trouble, and communicating accurately with families.

The new imaging technologies that form the body of research we refer to as early brain development provide us with a clear timetable for wiring opportunities (see page 20) in all four areas of development; cognitive, social, emotional, and physical.

The developmental norms for each area of development are listed on pages 24–26. Remember, these norms are guidelines only and will vary from child to child. The age categories are overlapping in an attempt to illustrate the great range of individual skill development.

Age	Skills
Birth to 4 months	Displays sensory awareness--see, hear, taste, smell, feel
	Develops distance vision: at birth--9–14 inches, at 1 month--1–2 feet, at 3 months--6–8 feet
	Cries to express needs
	Enjoys social interactions
	Begins to turn head
	Makes eye contact
	Makes cooing sounds
	Smiles
	Lifts head to look around
	Turns head toward a familiar voice
	Grasps a small object
	Tracks an object moving from side to side
3 months to 7 months	Reaches
	Expresses happiness and sadness
	Supports upper body with arms when on stomach
	Looks at hands and feet
	Bats or hits at an object
	Enjoys looking in a mirror
	Rolls over
	Recognizes familiar people
	Plays "Peek-a-Boo"
	Laughs
	Attempts to pull up
	Bounces when standing in an adult's lap
	Holds a bottle
6 months to 10 months	Sits unassisted
	Looks for an items when dropped
	Looks for an item when hidden under a pillow
	Drops things on purpose
	Changes an object from one hand to the other
	Rocks on hands and knees
	Mimics actions
	Mimics sounds
	Babbles a string of sounds
	Pulls up to a standing position
	Makes purposeful noise
	Puts small items in mouth

	Feeds self finger foods
	Looks at pictures when named
	Picks things up
	Pushes and shoves things
	Crawls
9 months to 13 months	Recognizes familiar words
	Takes off clothing
	Fits nesting boxes together
	Waves goodbye
	Crawls, scoots, creeps
	Follows simple directions
	Looks at a book
	Remembers where familiar items are kept
	Drops thing into an open box
	Scoops items
	Begins to roll a ball
	Babbles, mimicking speech
	Tears paper
	Copies simple gestures
	Scribbles
	Approximates simple words
12 months to 19 months	Moves around the room
	Plays simple pretend games
	Puts items in and take them out of a container
	Uses one-word sentences
	Plays simple musical instruments
	Hands items to someone
	Helps dress and undress self
	Rolls a ball
	Uses identification words correctly
	Enjoys looking at a book
	Retrieves ball that has rolled out of sight
	Walks upstairs with help
	Notes differences in temperature, smell, and taste
	Attempts to sing a song
	Enjoys messy play
	Points at familiar objects
	Hugs and kisses
	Recognizes self in mirror

	Stacks two or more blocks
	Turns two or three pages of a book at a time
	Tries to kick a ball
	Shows one or more body parts
	Pushes, pulls, or carries a toy while walking
	Places pegs in holes
	Uses a spoon to scoop
18 months to 24 months	Throws a ball
	Attempts walking up and down stairs
	Shows a variety of emotions
	Chews food
	Zips and unzips
	Points to several body parts
	Walks on wide balance board
	Rides a small riding toy
	Enjoys nursery rhymes and songs
	Says two-word sentences
	Unwraps packages with help
	Matches sounds to animals
	Turns book pages one at a time
	Enjoys water play
	Sings words of a song (at least some)
	Attempts to jump in place
	Repeats words you say
	Works a simple puzzle
	Strings large beads
	Uses playdough
	Uses finger paint
	Holds pictures right side up
	Uses words that tell what an object does
	Recognizes self in a picture
	Runs
	Listens to a short story
	Tries to balance on one foot

Family Partnerships

Family members are your partners. Therefore, it is critical to establish communication procedures that make it possible for family members to tell you about important events that occur in the infant's life at home each night or over a weekend, and, in return, you communicate what the infant experiences during the day. Infants are completely unable to provide this information to either their family members or to you. Here are some suggestions for maintaining effective communication with families:

1. Develop family communication forms (see pages 236–238) that travel home and back to school again. These forms should contain information regarding the infant's food intake, sleeping patterns, and general mood. It can also provide a space to share special small or large accomplishments or cute things that the child did that day. Families miss a lot during the day, and you miss a lot during the evening. The communication forms help everyone feel that they are in tune with the infant.

2. Place a bulletin board in an area of the room that is accessible to family members as they pick up their children. Use the bulletin board to inform families of upcoming events, to share information regarding infant development, to announce special activities that occur during the day ("Look What We Did Today!"), and to inform families of family education opportunities.

3. Provide a family library. Include special articles on infant care and development, books about infant growth and development, and pamphlets and brochures from local and state childcare agencies.

4. As much as possible, try to talk with each child's family every day. Share critical information but don't forget to pass on information about the clever and cute things their children do during the day.

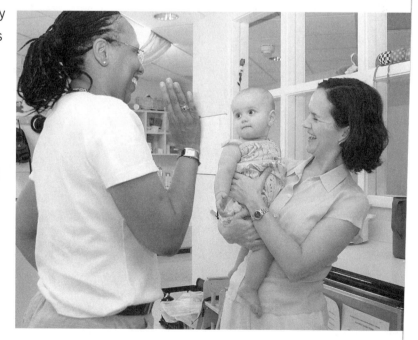

Using This Book

The Complete Resource Book for Infants is a collection of more than 700 easy-to-implement experiences and activities that maximize learning and development for children birth to 18 months. Experiences and activities are designed to support language, motor, social, emotional, and cognitive growth and development. Activities are structured around the windows of opportunity as defined by early brain development research. They can be used randomly or they can be organized to focus on a specific skill or aspect of development.

The appendix of *The Complete Resource Book for Infants* is filled with songs, fingerplays, chants, rhymes, games, recipes for food, recipes for art, and simple directions for teacher-made games and activities—plenty of things that babies love to do.

There are additional tools in the appendix to help you enhance your classroom and your curriculum: songs, rhymes and chants, stories, games, dances, and recipes; family communication tools; American Sign Language signs; lists of books, CDs, toys, equipment and materials; a developmental checklist, and resources for caregivers.

The first three years are the most critical time for development in the human lifespan. This book offers ways to use every opportunity to maximize the potential of every child. You hold in your hands the capability to shape a young child's future. What an awesome responsibility!

Chapter 1

Language Development—
Connecting With the World

Overview

There is no more fertile time in life for developing language than the first few years. Auditory discrimination and auditory memory are wired during an infant's first year of life. Infants' sensitivity to sound is present at birth. They begin to make sounds within the first week of life. By six weeks, they begin to control the sounds they make. However, language is a complex system that evolves throughout life.

Infants need a language-rich environment filled with sounds and people who talk to them, read to them, and sing to them. Their ability to learn language is largely an auditory experience but hearing sounds alone will not be enough. The sounds of language must be accompanied by the opportunity to visually watch the speaker's mouth as she says the sounds. The lip patterns associated with sounds such as "eee" and "ooo" will serve as an important clue. Infants also need to hear language in context to actually internalize vocabulary. For example, *I am going to pick you up* provides a clue for understanding the significance of the word *up*.

The Sounds of Language—Awareness of Sounds

Infants form native language maps during the first year of life. A neuron is assigned to every sound they hear between the fourth and eighth month of life. The more we read to them, talk to them, and sing to them, the more exact their language maps will be. The more people who read, speak, and sing to them, the better. Each person's voice is distinct, and the exposure to a variety of dialects and accents as well as the exposure to sounds in general allows the brain to refine the sounds it is storing. The accurateness of this early language map lays a foundation for later ability to discriminate the subtle differences between the sounds made by the letters "b" and "d" when formal reading instruction is encountered. (Gopnik, Meltzoff, and Kuhl, 2001)

Vocabulary

Children are also receptive to developing vocabulary (words that they can say) during the first few years of life. By the age of 18 months, a child who has been around a chatty caretaker will have 185 more vocabulary words than a peer in a "not so chatty" environment. By the time that child is two, the increase in vocabulary will be 295 words. (Huttenlocher et al, 1991)

The Caregiver's Role

Because the size of a child's vocabulary and his ability to discriminate sounds are two of the most acclaimed predictors of how easily he will learn to read, it makes sense that caregivers take the responsibility of building a solid foundation very seriously. Building an awareness of sounds and developing vocabulary are the primary goals of language development in the infant environment.

How will we accomplish these goals? Exposure to language is the way to build language. Appropriate experiences for infants include conversations (often one way), songs, rhymes, fingerplays, and stories. Research indicates that these experiences will enhance both the structure and the capacity of this wiring for language development.

If you want to assist a child with early literacy skills—sing, sing, sing, read, read, read, and talk, talk, talk to him.

Experiences and Activities to Create an Awareness of Sounds

Birth–18+Months

Sound Words to Know. Use vocabulary words related to sounds. Use the words in the chart below as often as you can.

Books About Sounds. Read books that explore sounds. Here are some favorites:

Babble	Hear	Pleasant	Splash
Beat	High	Rattle	Splish
Blow	Hum	Read	Squeak
Chant	Instruments	Rhyme	Suck
Clap	Laugh	Scream	Tap
Coo	Loud	Sing	Unpleasant
Cry	Low	Soft	Voice
Ears	Music	Sounds	Whisper
Giggle	Noise	Speak	

Barnyard Banter by Denise Fleming

Moo-Baa-La, La, La by Sandra Boynton

Old MacDonald Had a Farm by Rosanne Litzinger

Pudgy Book of Mother Goose Rhymes by Richard Walz

The Wheels on the Bus by Todd South

Sing, Sing, Sing. Sing songs every day. Sing traditional songs. Sing songs you make up on the spur of the moment. Singing songs with rhyming words is great, but babies don't know the difference. Don't let the words keep you from singing about whatever is going on. Several simple songs are provided in the appendix (pages 186–198).

Chomp, Chomp. Talk with children about the sounds that they make as they eat. *When you chew a cracker, it makes a crunching sound.*

Nonsense Rhymes. Make up nonsense rhyming word chants for each child's name. Use the chants with infants during diaper changing time, feeding time, or as a special morning greeting. *Hey, hey Katie, aidie, batie, sadie, my matie* or *Hey, hey Gabrielle, sabrielle, fabrielle, my belle.*

Nursery Rhyme Chatter. Recite nursery rhymes (appendix pages 204–215) to children throughout the day.

THE COMPLETE RESOURCE BOOK FOR INFANTS

Hear the Beat. Play a variety of music, such as classical, country, blues, jazz, and so on, during play time. Provide rattles to shake or boxes to beat so that older children can tap or shake to the tempo of the music.

Pitter-Patter. Call attention to the sound of rain as it hits the windows. *It is raining*

outside. Can you hear the rain? What sound is the rain making? Pitter-patter, pitter-patter. When outdoors, call attention to the sound of the wind as it rustles the leaves on the trees. *What sound is the wind making? Swoosh. Shhhh.*

Whispering. Whisper to infants during diaper changing time or during play time. Hold one of the baby's hands in front of your mouth so that he can feel your breath on his fingers. Sing a song in a whisper. Sing a song in your normal voice. Call his name in a whisper. Call his name in your normal voice.

Turn Up the Volume. Start singing a song in a whisper and gradually increase the volume of your voice.

Listening Walk. Take infants outdoors for a walk. Discuss all the sounds you hear on your walk. For example, *I hear the cars. Listen to the sound of the tires. You can tell which* *cars are moving fast and which ones are moving slowly.* It is not important that infants understand everything you say. Older infants will be listening to the sounds you point out. Younger babies will enjoy the sound of your voice. Here is a rhyme to accompany your walk.

Listening Walk by Pam Schiller
Going for a walk is so much fun.
We don't hurry and we don't run.
We look at all the pretty trees
And listen for birds and buzzing bees.

Wind Chimes. Hang wind chimes outdoors. When infants are outdoors, talk with them about the sounds the chimes make.

I Hear My Name. Sing songs with children's names in them, such as "This Is Tiffany" or say chants such as "Hello, Friends." Infants will begin to recognize their names sometime around six months. They will love hearing their names pop up in the middle of a song.

This Is Tiffany by Pam Schiller (Tune: Here We Go 'Round the Mulberry Bush)
This is Tiffany over here, over here.
She has on a bright blue dress.
This is Tiffany, our new friend.
We're so glad she's here.

Hello Friends
Hello, good friend.
Hello, good friend.
How are you, Kathy?

Birth–6 Months

"Parentese." Talk with babies using a high-pitched, singsong voice. This is a natural voice to use with infants. Some experts call it "parentese" because it seems to be instinctive for mothers and fathers, and really all adults, to use this type of voice as they talk to infants. Babies are particularly attentive when listening to a message delivered in a high-pitched, singsong voice.

A Message From Home. Ask a family member to record a song. Play the tape for the baby. Talk about the sound of the familiar voice. *Who is that? Do you recognize that voice? Is that your daddy?*

Hum a Tune. Hold the infant with his head on your shoulder and hum a tune. Use tunes that have variations in tempo and pitch.

Where Is It? Shake a rattle behind the baby, just out of sight. Does he turn to find it?

Baby Talk Translations. When infants begin to coo, talk back to them. Make a statement about what they might be saying—*I know you are telling me how happy you are today* or *I bet you are telling me what you want for lunch.*

Rhyme Talk. Encourage the baby to grasp your finger. Talk about how strong his hands are and how tight his grasp is getting. Use one of the following rhymes if you wish or make up a rhyme of your own.

> **Your Fingers Grow Stronger** by Pam Schiller
> Your fingers grow stronger every day.
> I feel them when we hold hands.
> I feel them when we play.
> Think of all the things you can do.
> Hold a rattle, point to a friend,
> And soon pick up a pea, tie a shoe.

> **Holding Tight**
> With your left hand you hold my finger oh so tight.
> Now, let's see if you can do it with your right.

Baby Sounds. Record the baby as he babbles and coos. Play the tape back for him. Does he respond to the familiar sounds?

Squeaky Toys. Place soft latex squeak toys around the baby. Show him how to squeeze the toys. Describe the sounds as he squeaks the toys.

Copy Cat Sounds. Locate two soft latex squeaky toys—one for the baby and one for you. Squeeze your toy and wait for baby to squeeze his. Squeeze your toy twice and see if the baby copies. As the baby learns to follow, try simple patterns—two quick squeaks, and then two quick squeaks, pause, long squeak.

Squeak, Squeak. Hand the baby two soft latex squeak toys—one for each hand. Can he squeak both toys at the same time?

Is That Me? Record the sounds of baby babbling and cooing. Play it back to the baby. Does he recognize his voice? Does he stop to listen? Do his eyes light up?

Ba-Ba-Ba-Ba. Sing "Twinkle, Twinkle, Little Star" using "ba-ba-ba-ba" instead of words. Try the song using other babbling sounds, such as da-da, ma-ma, pa-pa, and so on. Remember that babies are forging neural connections for sounds between the fourth and eighth months of life. This is the absolute best time to offer them experiences with phonetic sounds (Gopnik et al, 2001). Sing other familiar songs, exchanging letter sounds for words.

Tongue Twisters. Recite tongue twisters to babies. They are very receptive to sounds. Of course, they won't know what you are saying but the repetitive sounds will be helpful to their development.

6–12 Months

Find the Music. Place a musical toy under a blanket. Does the baby look for it? Encourage him to do so. Where is the sound coming from? Use your ears to find the sound.

Musical Toys. Surround the infant with musical toys. Play the toys one at a time. Play the toys all at the same time. Describe the musical sounds to infants as you play them. That phone has a high ring. The elephant makes a trumpeting sound.

Distance Conversation. When you are busy with other children, talk to the infant from across the room. Call the child's name and repeat it often as you talk. *Hi, Evan. I hear you playing. I'm over here changing Megan's diaper. I see Evan is having fun with that truck. Can you make it move across the floor?* When infants hear voices from varying distances it helps refine their auditory perception.

Routine Chants. Make up chants about daily activities and use them often with children. For example, you might make up a chant about changing a baby's diaper.

> **Here I Come Chant**
> Here I come, Sweetie Pie.
> In just a minute you'll be dry.

The rhythmic structure of language is appealing to infants. It encourages them to listen attentively.

Silly Sounds. Make silly sound and encourage the infant to copy the sounds you make. Try "raspberries," tongue clicks, air puffs, and lip vibrations. If the baby makes new sounds, try to copy them.

Service Please. Place a service bell on the infant's tray during lunchtime or snack time. Baby can ring the bell between bites. **Safety Note:** Supervise babies' use of service bells.

Jingle-Jangle. Place jingle bells inside empty, clean, clear plastic bottles and glue on the lids. Encourage infants to roll the bottles across the floor.

Sound Vibrations. Place the infant's hands on your mouth as you repeat his favorite sounds. He will feel the vibrations of the sounds you are making. Place his hand on his mouth and he will feel the vibrations of his sounds.

Sound-in-a-Box. Talk to the baby with a box over your head. Say a few words or sing a few lines of a song. Then, remove the box and repeat the words or song. Infants like to watch your mouth move, but they also enjoy the variation of sound that the box creates.

Alliterative Names. Make up alliterative names for babies. For example, Terrific Tiffany, Quality Quinn, Easy Evan, Kind Kira, and Marvelous Matthew. Use their alliterative names several times during the day.

Environmental Sounds. Infants enjoy listening to the many sounds of nature. Play tapes or CDs of environmental sounds. Some nature soundtracks have the sounds of running water, rain, birds singing, crickets chirping, thunder, ocean waves, and other sounds.

A Second Language. If you are able, sing or talk to babies in a second language. Teach them to count. Sing a simple song. Teach them how to say hello and goodbye. Children are highly receptive to the sounds of all languages during the first year of life. If they hear the sounds often enough they will form language maps for the second language, which means when they formally learn the language later in life they will be able to speak the language without accent or dialect (Kotulak, 1993; Nash, 1997).

12–18+ Months

Funny Sounds. Take turns making funny sounds with an infant, such as "raspberries," clucks, and smacks. *That is a funny sound! Can you make a loud sound? That was very loud!*

Interpretations. When babies make a familiar sound that sounds like a word, say the word back to them. Make a connection between what they are attempting to say and the object when possible. For example, when the infant says *ba-ba*, hand him a bottle and then say, *Ba-ba. Do you want your bottle? Here is your bottle.*

Funny Names. Use funny-sounding names for infants' body parts. For example, you might use some of the following:

Head Bumper	Chin Chopper
Nose Blower	Ear Hearer
Eye Winker	Tooters (feet)
Mouth Muncher	Piggies (toes)

Use these funny terms when playing with babies. *I'm going to get your Nose Blower. What a cute little Chin Chopper! Let's put the food in your Mouth Muncher. I love these little Piggies.*

Tick Tock. Hide a clock with a loud ticking sound. Invite infants to find the clock by using their ears. As they become skilled in finding the clock, hide it in more challenging hiding places.

Megaphones. Give infants empty toilet paper rolls and show them how to use them as megaphones. Demonstrate singing, whispering, speaking, and humming through the "megaphones."

Musical Hide and Seek. Hide a musical toy and let infants find it with their ears. Ask them questions about how they found the toy. *I wonder how we can find the toy. How do we know where to look? How do we know when we are getting close?*

Animal Sounds. Collect an assortment of rubber animals or animal pictures. Teach children the sounds that each animal makes. Older children will be able to imitate the sounds.

Old MacDonald. Sit on the floor with one or two children. Sing, "Old MacDonald Had a Farm." Show pictures of each animal as it is mentioned in the song. Older children may be able to make the sounds for the animals without your help.

Nursery Rhyme Time. Recite familiar nursery rhymes. The rhyming word patterns and the rhythm of the text in nursery rhymes are enchanting to children of all ages. Nursery rhymes help children develop an ear for sound and an appreciation of the role cadence plays in language. After reciting a rhyme a few times, stop on the second word in a rhyming word pair and see if your "talkers" can fill in the word. Say the rhyme and whisper the rhyming words. See appendix pages 204–215 for a selection of simple nursery rhymes.

Songs With Sounds. Sing other songs with sounds incorporated into them, such as "Six White Ducks" and "Wheels on the Bus." Older infants will sing along and younger children will soon be able to make some of the sounds.

Six White Ducks

Six white ducks that I once knew,
Fat ducks, skinny ducks, they were, too.
But the one little duck with the feather on her back,
She ruled the others with a quack, quack, quack!

Down to the river they would go,
Wibble, wobble, wibble, wobble all in a row.
But the one little duck with the feather on her back,
She ruled the others with a quack, quack, quack!

Wheels on the Bus

The wheels on the bus go round and round. (move hands in circular motion)
Round and round, round and round.
The wheels on the bus go round and round,
All around the town. (extend arms up and out)

Additional Verses:
The wipers on the bus go swish, swish, swish... (sway hands back and forth)
The baby on the bus goes, "Wah, wah, wah..." (rub eyes)
People on the bus go up and down... (stand up, sit down)
The horn on the bus goes beep, beep, beep... (pretend to beep horn)
The money on the bus goes clink, clink, clink... (drop change in)
The driver on the bus says, "Move on back..." (move arm in hitchhiking movement)

Jingle Bell Blocks. Prepare Jingle Bell Blocks (appendix page 229). Encourage the little builders to build with the blocks. Discuss the sounds the blocks make when you pick them up and when you knock them down.

Vroom. Make the sounds that accompany some of the classroom toys, such as cars and trucks go *vroom*, dogs *pant* and *bark*, cats *meow*, phones *ring*, clocks *tick* and so on. You will be rewarded soon when children begin to make the sounds of classroom toys as they play.

Splash. Give the children sponge balls to toss into a shallow tub of water. Point out the sound of the water splashing in the tub.

Echo Songs. Sing echo songs. You sing a line and a second caregiver echoes your line. Encourage the infants to "sing" along. Any song will work, such as "Twinkle, Twinkle Little Star," "Itsy Bitsy Spider," or "Mary Had a Little Lamb."

Twinkle, Twinkle, Little Star
Twinkle, twinkle, little star,
How I wonder what you are!
Up above the world so high,
Like a diamond in the sky.
Twinkle, twinkle, little star,
How I wonder what you are!

Itsy Bitsy Spider
The itsy bitsy spider
Went up the waterspout.
Down came the rain,
And washed the spider out.
Out came the sun,
And dried up all the rain.
And the itsy bitsy spider
Went up the spout again.

Mary Had a Little Lamb
Mary had a little lamb, little lamb, little lamb.
Mary had a little lamb,
Her fleece was white as snow.

Everywhere that Mary went, Mary went, Mary went,
Everywhere that Mary went
The lamb was sure to go.

Hummingbirds. Many infants can learn to hum songs long before they are able to sing them. Hum familiar tunes, such as "Twinkle, Twinkle, Little Star" and "Itsy Bitsy Spider" frequently. You will be surprised one day when infants hum along.

Voice Variations. Demonstrate how you can change the sound of your voice by talking into a paper cup, a glass, a coffee can, a trashcan, a paper box, or another object in the classroom.

Ball Drum Sounds. Place a large ball on the carpet and slap it with your hand. *The ball makes a soft sound on the carpet.* Encourage the infants to hit the ball and listen to the sound. Move the ball to an uncarpeted area and again hit it like a drum. *The ball makes a different sound on the floor.* Invite the infants to try hitting the ball on different surfaces, such as a blanket, a pillow, or a table.

Character Voices. Read a short version of "The Three Little Pigs." Use dramatic character voices for the pigs and the wolf.

Hop, Hop, Stop. Say *"Hop, hop, stop!"* and encourage infants to hop when you say *hop* and stop when you say *stop*. Change the number of hops before saying stop to keep babies listening for the stop.

Fee-Fi-Fo-Fum. Encourage the infants to stomp around the room as you say the following "Fee-Fi-Fo-Fum" chant.

Fee-Fi-Fo-Fum
Fee-Fi-Fo-Fum,
Fee-Fi-Fo-Fum,
Fee-Fi-Fo-Fum,
Rum Tum Tum!

Chants, Chants, Chants. Babies love chants, especially simple ones that they can clap to, jump with, or repeat easily. The appendix has several chants (see appendix pages 204–215). Here are a few favorites.

Clickety, Clickety, Clack
Clickety, clickety, clack.
Clickety, clickety, clack.
Clickety, clickety, clickety, clickety,
Clickety, clickety clack.

Ice Cream Chant
You scream.
I scream.
We all scream for ice cream.

18+ Months

Tone Bottles. Fill four or five glasses with varying levels of water. Tap each glass and talk about the sounds that result. Invite infants to help you arrange the glasses in order from highest to lowest. **Safety Note:** Supervise closely.

Sound Maker. Fill a spray bottle with a small amount of water. Gather a variety of surfaces, such as a cookie sheet, shower curtain, towel, and so on. Spray the surfaces with different pressures of water and discuss the sounds that the water makes when it hits each surface. *Point to the one that makes the loudest sound. Which one makes no sound?* Older infants may be able to spray the bottle themselves.

Color to the Beat. Play some classical music and invite the infants to color to the beat of the music. Some babies will naturally follow the beat; others may appear to hear nothing. Sit beside babies and color with them. Try changing the beat of the music.

Can Telephones. Provide Can Telephones (appendix page 225) for infants to use as they babble and talk. Consider pairing infants with each other or with an adult. Do the babies catch on to when and how to talk and when and how to listen?

Kazoos. Make kazoos (appendix page 230). Demonstrate how to play the homemade kazoo and encourage the little musicians to play kazoos of their own.

I Hear Footsteps. Provide a variety of shoes, such as slippers, sneakers, hard-sole shoes, and so on, to explore. Invite infants to walk across the floor in each type of shoe. Discuss the sounds that the different types of shoes make. *Which shoes make the loudest sound? Which make the softest sound?*

Little Sir Echo. Tell the baby that you are going to play a name game. Explain that you will call his name and he should call yours in return. Call his name in a low voice and wait for him to call yours. Call his name in a high-pitched voice and wait for him to call yours. Whisper baby's name and wait for him to call yours. It may take a while for baby to catch on to the changes in voices but he will, and when he does, he will use his many voices to call you.

Second-Language Sounds. Use a variety of languages to say hello and goodbye. Babies develop an ear for the sounds of any language they encounter during the first few years of life.

Language	Hello	Goodbye
Spanish	hola	adios
French	bonjour, allo	adieu
Afrikaans	dag, hallo	tot siens
Italian	buongiorno, ciao	arrivederci

Experiences and Activities to Develop Vocabulary

Birth–18+ Months

Vocabulary Words. Use words related to vocabulary when appropriate and as often as you can with babies. Here are a few suggestions.

Communicate	Opposites
Describe	Signs
Explain	Speak
Expressions	Talk
Language	Understand
New	Words

Books That Build Vocabulary. Read books that introduce vocabulary words. Here are some favorites:

Animal Kisses by Barney Saltzberg
Baby Food by Margaret Miller
Baby Pets by Margaret Miller
Brown Bear, Brown Bear, What Do You See? by Bill Martin, Jr.
The Foot Book by Dr. Seuss
Goodnight Moon by Margaret Wise Brown
One Fish, Two Fish by Dr. Seuss
Opposites by Sandra Boynton
Pat the Bunny by Dorothy Kunhardt

Mystery Box. Make a Mystery Box (appendix page 231). Decorate a box with bright colors and intriguing patterns. Add a few question marks. Each week place three or four items of interest in the box, such as stuffed animals, brightly colored bags, toys from the classroom, or other objects. Take the items out one at a time and introduce them to the children. Use the name of the item several times. Ask the infants who are able to talk to repeat the name of the item. Place all the items out for the children to explore. Focus on the names of these items as vocabulary for the day or for the week.

A Picture Encourages My Words. Collect simple photos, posters, or magazine pictures to use with the children. The less clutter in the picture the more able infants will be to focus on specific items in the picture. Laminate the pictures if possible. Talk with the children about the pictures. Posters can be placed in the feeding or diaper areas, on the walls, or into plastic sleeves and in three-ring binders for further observation.

Baggie Books. Make a classroom photo baggie book (appendix page 226) and change the pictures in the book on a regular basis. Sit with children individually and discuss the various pictures. *Point to the red color on this page. Are there any people on this page? Are there animals in the pictures?* Encourage older infants to tell you what they see.

Look Through Books. Look through books and ask infants to point to and name illustrations on each page. Ask older infants to point to objects on the page.

That's Interesting! Wear a lei or carnival bead necklace around your neck. At diaper changing time or feeding time talk to baby about the decoration around your neck. Describe the item. Talk about the colors, texture, and other features of the necklace.
Overhead Streamers. Hang colorful streamers over the changing table. Discuss the

streamers with the baby while you are changing his diaper. Talk about the colors of the streamers, how they move with the breeze, and how long they are.

I Know That Voice. Ask family members to record themselves reading a short book, telling a story, or singing a song. Play the recording for infants during quiet times.

Bringing the Outside In. Take an infant to a window. Talk to him about the interesting things you see outdoors. *What is the weather like? Are there people outside? What color are the flowers? Are animals passing by?*

Talk Walks. Take babies outdoors for a walk. Discuss what you see and how the weather feels. *Look at those birds. I think they are looking for food. It is cool outside today. I like this kind of weather.*

What's This? Keep a basket or box of safe, interesting items by the diaper-changing table. Give the baby an item to hold while you change his diaper. Talk to him about the item he is holding.

Diaper-Changing Vocabulary. When changing an infant's diaper, use vocabulary that relates to your actions. You will find that your descriptions of what you are doing will provide a meaningful way to introduce the concept of opposites. You place baby on the changing table and take him off the table when you are finished. You change a wet diaper to a dry diaper. You take the old diaper off and put on a new one. If the child is able to walk, you will pick him up and put him down when you are finished.

Feely Cylinders. Make Feely Cylinders (appendix page 228). Give them to infants to

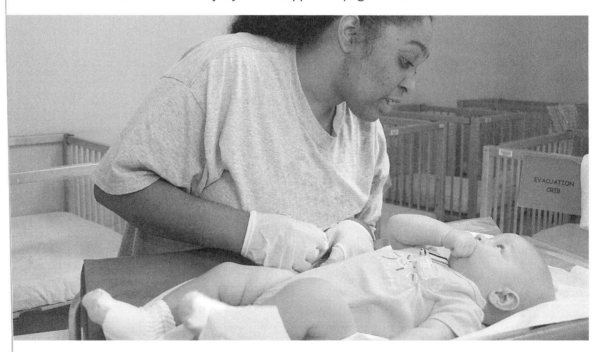

explore. They are just right for tiny hands. Discuss the feel of each cylinder. Roll the cylinders on the babies' hands, arms, and cheeks.

Birth–6 Months

Clothing Descriptions. Talk to infants about the clothing they are wearing. *I love the flowers on your dress, Madison. Austin, what big stripes you have on your shirt!* Talk to them about what you are wearing.

Textured Bottle Wraps. Make Textured Bottle Wraps (appendix page 235). Talk with the baby about how different his bottle feels. Describe the texture of the cloth.

Here Are My Hands. When the infant begins to look at his hands, talk with him about what he sees. *Those are your tiny fingers. You have five fingers on each hand. Here are your little fingernails. Those are such sweet hands.* Recite "Little Hands" to him.

> **Little Hands** by Pam Schiller
> Little hands, sweet hands.
> Hands to do so much.
> Hands to hold.
> Hands to touch.
> Little hands, sweet hands,
> Hands to do so much.

Here Are My Feet. Dye or purchase socks in bright colors. Sew on some bows and some bells. Be creative. Place the socks on the infant's feet once in a while to provide a change of scenery. Talk to the baby about his feet and his brightly colored socks. Look at your bright socks! I see pretty red bows. Do you see the red bows? Make up a rhyme to say to him, or use the one below. **Safety Note:** Supervise closely to make sure that bows and other decorations don't come loose.

> **Feet Rhyme** by Pam Schiller
> One foot, two feet,
> Isn't that neat?
> One foot, two feet,
> Isn't that sweet?

Soft Talk. Talk to the baby about how soft his skin feels. Talk to him about his soft hair. Rub the baby's hands on your skin and talk about how it feels. Run his fingers through your hair. Talk about the textures that he feels.

Up and Down. Lift baby up over your head and then down again as you say the following rhyme.

> **Up and Down** by Pam Schiller
> Up, up you go, over my head.
> Down, down you come under my chin.
> Now up, up over my head again.

Here We Go. Say the following chant "Here We Go" and move children around as directed by the words of the chant.

> **Here We Go** by Pam Schiller
> Here we go—up, up, up.
> Here we go—down, down, down.
> Here we go—moving forward.
> Here we go—moving backward.
> Here we go 'round and 'round and 'round.

Drink Your Milk. Sing to infants as they are drinking their bottles. You can sing anything or make up a tune. Here is a tune about drinking milk that is sung to the tune of "Row, Row, Row Your Boat."

> **Drink, Drink, Drink Your Milk** by Pam Schiller
> Drink, drink, drink your milk
> A little at a time.
> Drink it slow, drink it fast,
> Drink it to this rhyme.

Bounce Baby. Hold the baby on your lap and gently bounce him while saying the following rhyme, "Bounce, Baby, Bounce." Reinforce the words *bounce*, *up*, and *back* by stressing them with your voice.

> **Bounce, Baby, Bounce** by Pam Schiller
> Bounce, baby, bounce.
> Bounce, baby, bounce.
> Bounce up.

Bounce back.
Bounce, baby, bounce.
Bounce, baby, bounce.
Bounce right into my arms.

Mobile Delights. Hang a mobile over the diaper-changing area. Talk about the items on the mobile while you are changing diapers. Change the mobile for another one after a couple of weeks.

Mirror Talk. Sit in front of a mirror with the infant in your lap facing the mirror. Talk to him about his eyes, ears, nose, mouth, hair, arms, fingers, and so on. *You have two bright and happy eyes, a sweet little button nose, and a cute little rosebud mouth. You are beautiful.*

Talking Toys. Provide talking toys for babies. Repeat what the toy says to them.

6–12 Months

Texture Talk. Give the baby a piece of textured cloth, such as burlap, silk, or vinyl, to hold while you are changing his diaper or giving him a bottle. Talk about how the cloth feels. *This cloth feels soft, and this one feels prickly. Feel this soft cloth. Feel this scratchy cloth.*

Something to Talk About. Pick an interesting toy from the toy box. Hold the infant on your lap and look closely at the toy. Describe the toy in detail. *This toy is blue and yellow and it is shaped like a square. When you shake it, you can hear the bell inside.*

Family Roll-Overs. Make Family Roll-Overs (appendix page 227). Talk about the pictures on the canisters. Describe the people in the photos or the activities going on in the pictures.

Colorful Mats. Lay the infant on a colorful mat or beach towel. Talk about the designs and colors on the mat.

Interesting Scenery. Secure stuffed animals, rattles, colorful pictures, and other interesting objects on the floor and on table and chair legs. Get down on the floor with the babies and crawl with them along the path you have enhanced. Stop and note interesting items.

Texture Talk. Collect several textured items and place them in a bag or basket. Sit with the infant. Hand him one item at a time. Talk about what the item is and how it feels.

Gentle Hands. Talk about using "gentle hands" when children get rowdy or approach a toy or child aggressively. This will be a concept that will take time to develop but now is the time to begin introducing the concept. Demonstrate using gentle hand and soft strokes.

6–12 Months

My Eyes Can See. Say the following rhyme "My Eyes Can See." Touch each part of the baby's body as it is mentioned in the rhyme.

> **My Eyes Can See** by Pam Schiller (suit actions to the words)
> My eyes can see.
> My mouth can talk.
> My ears can hear.
> My feet can walk.
> My nose can sniff,
> My teeth can chew.
> My lids can flutter,
> My arms hug you.

Puppet Play. Use puppets to talk with the babies. Use funny voices. Sing a song. Say a rhyme.

Upside Down Face. Position yourself so infants can get a view of your face upside down. Bend over and look through your legs. Talk with babies about how different your face looks. *Where are my eyes? Where is my mouth?*

Funny Clothes. Wear something unusual, such as a simple costume, large shirt, or special hat. Describe your clothing to the children.

Point to Your Eyes. Ask infants to point to their facial features and to items in the room. The ability to do this normally emerges around 11 months.

Where Is Big Toe! Sing "Where Is Thumbkin?" Changing "Thumbkin" to a body part. Not only does this song teach body parts, but it also demonstrates the reciprocal aspect ("your turn, my turn") of conversation.

Where Is Big Toe? adapted by Pam Schiller
Where is big toe?
Where is big toe?
Here I am!
Here I am!
How are you today, toe?
I am fine today, friend.
Wiggle, wiggle, wiggle.
Wiggle, wiggle, wiggle.

Additional verses:
Kneecap...bend, bend, bend.
Elbow...bend, bend, bend.
Bellybutton...poke, poke, poke.
Earlobe...pull, pull, pull.

Thelma Thumb. Recite "Thelma Thumb" and move the baby's thumb to the movements suggested in the rhyme. Older infants will be able to do the movements in the rhyme with you.

> **Thelma Thumb** (move thumb as directed)
> Thelma Thumb is up and Thelma Thumb is down.
> Thelma Thumb is dancing all around the town.
> Dance her on your shoulders, dance her on your head.
> Dance her on your knees and tuck her into bed.

Name other fingers: Phillip Pointer, Terry Tall, Richie Ring, Baby Finger, and Finger Family, and dance them on other body parts.

12–18+ Months

Funny Faces. Sit in front of a mirror with the baby and make funny faces. You may want to say the rhyme on the next page while examining your faces in the mirror. Discuss all part of the face. Point to the parts of the face on the baby and then to the parts of the face on yourself.

I Look in the Mirror by Pam Schiller
I look in the mirror and what do I see?
I see a funny face looking at me.
A scrunched up nose, twisted mouth, squinty eyes,
And two fuzzy eyebrows—what a surprise!
I look in the mirror and what do I do?
I giggle and laugh at the sight of me.

Hello. Provide play telephones or real phones that have been discarded. Pick a phone up as if it just rang. Say, *Hello, Kira. How are you? Yes, Austin is here. Do you want to talk to him? Here he is.* Hand Austin the phone.

Translating for Babies. Respond to simple word utterances by making them into a sentence, for example when a baby says wa wa, respond by saying Do you want a drink of water? As infants begin to talk, help them expand their sentences by responding to simple phrase such as, *see ball,* with *Would you like to have the ball?* Add names to a one-word utterance, such as, *Goodbye,* becomes, *Goodbye, Tamika*.

Hand Me the Block. Lay three or four familiar items on the floor. Ask the infant to hand you one of the items. For example, if you have a block, a rattle, a cup, and a book, ask the infant to hand you the block. Ask for each item individually until you have all the items. Change the items and do this activity often.

Texture Glove. Make a Texture Glove (appendix page 234). Put the glove on and invite the children to feel each finger of the glove. Talk about the feel of each finger. *Which finger is rough? Which one is smooth? Are any of the fingers bumpy?*

Photo Flappers. Make Photo Flappers (appendix page 232). Sit with infants and help them lift the flap. Talk about the pictures underneath the flaps.

Gigantic Star. Sing "Twinkle, Twinkle, Little Star" in a small voice with the infants. After singing the song once with the traditional words, sing it a second time and change the word "little" to "gigantic." Use your voice to indicate the difference between little and gigantic. Continue singing with new adjectives for the star.

Twinkle, Twinkle, Little Star
Twinkle, twinkle, little star,
How I wonder what you are!
Up above the world so high,
Like a diamond in the sky.
Twinkle, twinkle, little star,
How I wonder what you are!

A Word Here and There. Sing familiar songs with infants. Stop before words at the end of sentences and/or on special words and see if the children can fill in the word. If you do this activity often, you will be surprised at how well the babies will do. Often around 16 months of age, infants become quite interested in singing. If no one joins in, just keep singing. Someday, they will surprise you.

Name That Thing. Play a naming game with beginning talkers. Point to objects and say, "What's that?" Look through books and encourage infants to name things on each page.

Feed the Birds. Take dried bread or stale cereal outdoors to feed the birds. If you can go to a nearby lake you might even be able to take babies to feed the ducks. Note: Be sure the park allows feeding the birds. Talk with children about the birds or ducks. *Look at their feathers. Do you know that their mouth is called a beak or bill? What funny feet they have. Do you think they look like your feet? Can you walk like a bird/duck? Show me how birds/ducks walk*. Sing the following "Bird-Feeding Song" while you are feeding the birds or ducks.

> **Bird-Feeding Song adapted** by Pam Schiller (Tune: If You're Happy and
> You Know It)
> If you're hungry and you know it, flap your wings.
> If you're hungry and you know it, flap your wings.
> If you're hungry and you know it, your wings will surely show it.
> If you're hungry and you know it, flap your wings.
>
> If you're hungry and you know it...Shake your tail.
> If you're hungry and you know it ...shake your tail.

Recording Events. When you take a field trip or have a special day at school, record the event. Take photos and place them inside a Plastic Bag Book (appendix page 232). Make an appropriate cover with a title, such as Our Day at the Park, We Fed the Birds, and so on.

Big and Little Balls. Give the infants big balls and little balls. Talk with them while they play with the balls. Which balls are big? Where is a small ball? Do you like to play with the big ball or the small ball?

Follow That Car. Push a car around the floor and encourage the infants to follow you. Go under chairs, around table legs, and other places in the classroom. Describe the path you are taking as you go.

Photo Collections. Collect interesting photos. Sit with one or two infants and talk about the things in the pictures.

Teddy Bear Chant. Play "Teddy Bear, Teddy Bear" with infants.

> **Teddy Bear, Teddy Bear** (suit actions to the words)
> Teddy bear, teddy bear turn around.
> Teddy bear, teddy bear touch the ground.
> Teddy bear, teddy bear touch your shoe.
> Teddy bear, teddy bear say howdy-do.
> Teddy bear, teddy bear go up the stairs.
> Teddy bear, teddy bear say your prayers.
> Teddy bear, teddy bear turn out the light.
> Teddy bear, teddy bear say good night.

If You're Happy. Sing "If You're Happy and You Know It," changing the lyrics to elicit different movements from babies. For example, you might say *touch your toes* or *touch your nose.*

If You're Happy and You Know It

If you're happy and you know it, clap your hands. (clap hands twice)
If you're happy and you know it, clap your hands. (repeat)
If you're happy and you know it then your face will show it. (point to face)
If you're happy and you know it, clap your hands. (clap hands twice)

Reinforce Opposites. Opposites are patterns that help children make sense of their world. It is never too soon to start focusing on using opposite vocabulary. Below are examples of activities that teach two common pairs of opposites—in and out and on and off.

In and Out. Focus on the vocabulary words in and out. Here some suggestions for activities to demonstrate the meaning of the words.

- Toss a beanbag into a box. Discuss where it lands—*in* the box or *out* of the box.
- Invite infants to play with a laundry basket. Encourage them to get *in* the basket and when they are ready to get *out* of the basket, help them out as you verbally state that they are now *out of the basket*.
- Encourage babies to put a small object *in* a bucket and to dump the objects *out* of the bucket.
- Talk about the location of Jack when playing with a Jack-in-the-Box.

On and Off. Focus on the vocabulary words on and off. Here some suggestions for activities to demonstrate the meaning of the words.

- Place pieces of fabric or old towels on the floor. Have the infants step *on* and *off* the towels.
- Show the infants how the light switch works. Let them turn it *on* and *off*. Give them a flashlight and show them how to turn the light *on* and *off*.
- Tell the story of "The Three Billy Goats Gruff." Focus on the part of the story when the Troll says, *Who's that traipsing on my bridge?* and the part where he says, *Get off, get off, get off I say.*
- Give the children some hats to play with. Encourage them to put the hats *on* and then take them *off*. Talk with them while they play, reinforcing the vocabulary as you make suggestions for things they can do with the hats.

Do similar activities to reinforce other pairs of opposites, such as over/under, up/down, hot/cold, and so on.

Words and Actions. Clearly articulate the connections between gestures and words. For example, say, *Do you want to get down?* As you ask the question, point downward. Say, *Are you ready to go outside?* Point to the door.

Give infants beanbags and a basket. Show them how to toss the beanbag into the basket. Discuss the spot where the beanbag lands. *That one is* in *the basket. This one landed* out *of the basket.*

Point out places where infants spend time during the day—*in* his crib, *out* of his crib, *in* the classroom, *outside* on the playground, and so on.

I Spy. Play "I Spy" with infants. Keep it simple so they can be successful. *I spy something red. I spy something round that rolls on the floor. I spy a teacher.*

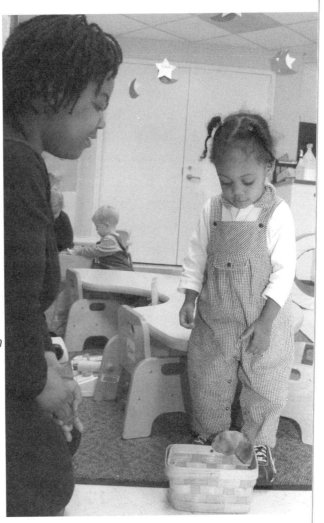

Noisy and Quiet Snacks. Provide some snack items that are noisy when chewed, such as crackers or apples, and others that are quiet (not noisy) when eaten, such as yogurt or gelatin.

I Can. Talk with infants about all the things they are learning to do. What things can they do with their hands? What can they do with their heads? What can they do with their faces? Share "I Can" with the little movers and shakers.

> **I Can** by Pam Schiller
> I can wave my hand—wave, wave, wave. (wave)
> I can shake my head—shake, shake, shake. (shake head yes and no)
> I can move around—move, move, move. (crawl or walk depending on ability)
> I can smile—ha, ha, ha. (smile)
> And I can blow you a kiss—smooch, smooch, smooch. (blow a kiss)

Vocabulary Check. Fill a small basket or box with three or four different items such as a ball, a squeeze toy, a spoon, and a cup. As you introduce each item to the children place it on the floor. When you are finished, place the items back in the basket. Ask individual children to hand you a specific item. How easily are they able to pick the one item out of the group? Who knows which thing is which?

Chant of Opposites. Make chants using pairs of opposites. Try to demonstrate the opposites as you chant. For example, say, *up and down—up and down—up and down—up and down,* while you pick the infant up and gently lay him down or while you watch a ball bounce up and down. Say, *on and off—on and off—on and off,* as you turn a flashlight on and off. Say, *in and out—in and out—in and out—in and out*, as you step in and out of a box or put the baby in and out of his carrier. Before you know it, he will be chanting the opposites with you.

18+ Months

Expanding Language. When infants begin to be able to put two words together, help them expand their vocabulary by gently nudging them to use their new ability. As children begin to be able to use language they will frequently ask for things using only one word. For example, when the baby says *up* to request being picked up, you say, *Do you want me to pick Rachel up?* The baby will probably shake his head *no. Oh, you want me to pick you up. Then say, "Pick me up, please." Then I will know it is you that you want picked up.* Water is another word that infants frequently use by itself. Say, *water? What do you want me to do with the water? Pour it on your head? Give it to Ms. Charner?* Reword the sentence to model the correct way to ask for water, *I would like a drink of water*.

Singing Circle. Sit on the floor each day and sing with babies. As they approach 18 months, they will begin to be interested in singing along. Sing simple songs such as "Mary Had a Little Lamb" and "Itsy Bitsy Spider." If you make this a daily routine, infants will come to expect it and will be more likely to participate.

Say and Touch. Play "Say and Touch." Encourage infants to participate.

> **Say and Touch** by Pam Schiller
> Say, "red" and touch your head.
> Say, "sky" and touch your eye.
> Say, "bear" and touch your hair.
> Say, "hear" and touch your ear.
> Say, "south" and touch your mouth.
> Say, "rose" and touch your nose.
> Say, "in" and touch your chin.
> Say, "rest" and touch your chest.
> Say, "farm" and touch your arm.
> Say, "yummy" and touch your tummy.
> Say, "bee" and touch your knee.
> Say, "neat" and touch your feet.

Magic Wand. Make a Magic Wand (appendix page 231). Encourage the infants to sit in a semicircle in front of you. Wave your wand with this magic incantation—*Willoughby, wallaby, woo, my wand is pointing to you.* Point the wand at a child and give that child a direction. For example, you might say, *touch your toes, stand up, point to your eyes, jump like a frog,* and so on.

Magic Box. Make a Magic Box (appendix page 230). Choose items to go inside that reflect the time of year or current interest in the classroom. Sit with the infants while they explore the items.

THE COMPLETE RESOURCE BOOK FOR INFANTS

Chapter 2

Social/Emotional Development
Becoming a Social Being

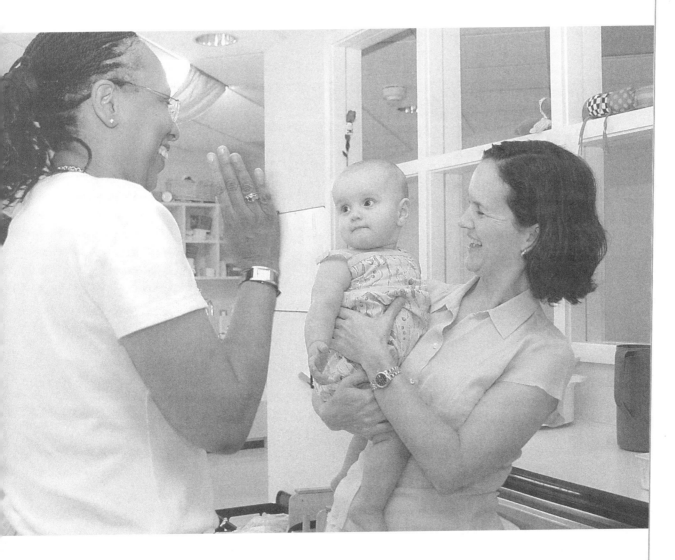

Overview

Building a Sense of Self

Infants begin to determine their place in the world during the first few weeks of life. To develop a positive sense of self right from the start, they must come to understand that they can cause good things to happen on a predictable basis. When they cry, you come. When they smile, you smile. Infants flourish when they experience an environment in which people respond positively to their needs and their efforts to elicit support and attention.

Infants discover their hands between the second and third months of life. An infant will look at her hands endlessly, until finally she understands that she can control them. From this point forward, she gradually discovers the many wonders of her body. She finds her feet and then becomes interested in locating her eyes, mouth, nose, and ears. With each discovery comes the knowledge of how the parts of her body can be used to exert her will.

A true sense of self develops between 15 and 18 months. Babies begin to express their opinions. They expand their emotions. They will show embarrassment, pride, shame, and guilt. They are now able to connect thoughts to actions and feelings. Some people call this period "the terrible twos" but that is not an accurate description. There will be tantrums, but most of them are easily resolved. A caregiver should be sensitive to an infant's inability to communicate her opinion and be ready to go the extra mile to try to interpret the infant's desires. This is where sign language really comes in handy.

It is important that babies become confident in their ability to take care of their needs. In a few short years, babies will move from total dependence on others to being well on the road to total independence. Our job is to help children on this incredible journey by always balancing their safety and well-being with their need for freedom to experiment and explore the world.

Developing Trust

The brain begins its job of wiring for emotional intelligence (well-being) soon after birth. The aspect of emotional intelligence that is wired during the first year of life is trust, which is the foundation for all social and emotional well-being. Trust is necessary for relationships with families, friends, and coworkers; it is impossible to develop self-confidence and self-competency without it. It is fundamental to becoming a self-actualized individual. When an infant experiences a warm, loving environment where her needs are met regularly, she learns to trust. If she experiences a hostile world where her needs are seldom met, she learns to mistrust (Ramey and Ramey, 1999).

Positive experiences in the infant classroom indicate that caregivers are responsive to infants' needs and are well trained in reading infants' cues (pages 21–22). Infants signal us when they are

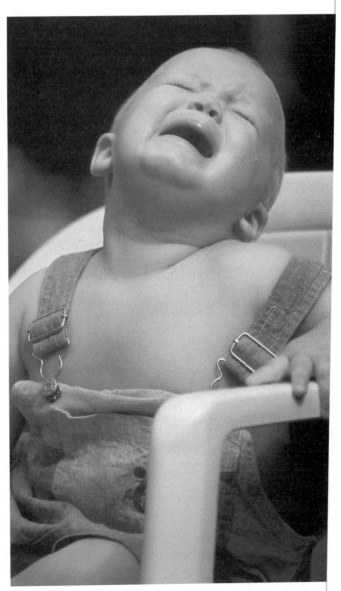

tired, when they are ready to learn, when they are frustrated, when they are uncomfortable, and when they are not feeling well. Most infants use standard cues; in addition, babies use cues unique to each of them. A responsive caregiver becomes skilled at reading both types of cues.

When babies signal distress or discomfort, soothe them. Research supports the notion that newborn babies can't be spoiled. There is no research that supports the idea that babies need to cry to exercise their lungs. When they are in distress (wet, hungry, tired, or in pain) they need to know that someone is there to help them. This is how they learn to trust others and to know that their needs are important. When babies are around six months old you can pull back a bit and let them realize that they can survive on their own. The first six months of responding to their needs will pay off because, deep down inside, they know someone cares.

It is difficult for infants to become accustomed to strangers. In a quality infant program, each infant is assigned to one primary caregiver. Along this same line of thinking, it is a good idea to limit the number of visitors allowed inside the infant classroom.

Babies thrive and their trust blooms when provided with warm, loving, and responsive care. They prosper when they are rocked, loved, spoken to, sung to, and held as often as they indicate a need.

Developing Impulse Control

Somewhere between the 16th and 18th months of life, babies come to understand that they have a will that is separate from yours. They begin to make demands and to express desires. You will notice that the child who always came indoors from outside time without a fuss suddenly expresses her desire to stay outside in such a dramatic way that it takes the form of a temper tantrum. At this point, the experiences infants encounter begin to forge the wiring for impulse control. They come to understand that there are boundaries that identify acceptable behavior and unacceptable behavior.

Setting rules and being consistent in following the rules will help infants identify the boundaries and wire behaviors that are within the limits of the boundaries. Inconsistency will lead to wiring connections that either result in an inability to control one's impulses or confusion about boundaries. Impulse control, along with trust, is at the heart of social-emotional stability. The right experiences at the right time will allow babies to develop control that will serve them well the rest of their lives.

Enhancing Social Interactions

Social and emotional development are equally as important as cognitive and physical development although, for the most part, they generally get much less attention. An infant begins wiring for healthy emotional intelligence and social responses from birth. The first two years of environmental influences and interactions with others will have a big impact on baby's lifelong social and emotional behaviors and attitudes (Ramey and Ramey, 1999).

The family is the source of an infant's first social and emotional experiences. The responses of family members are crucial to her sense of self and understanding of how she fits into her world (at this point her immediate family).

Babies develop an understanding of social nuances quickly. As early as one month, infants react emotionally to their environment. By four months, they are able to recognize differences in angry, happy, and expressionless faces. They will work to make you smile. Babies begin to laugh at four months. They respond to tickles and touches and by six months, they will begin to respond to simple games and anticipate your actions.

Socialization is broader than social development. It includes introducing infants to values, rules, and expectations within their immediate family, their classroom family, and eventually within their culture. A child's development of appropriate social and emotional skills will influence her success in school and eventually her success at work. It will influence her friendships and how others view her.

Developing Humor

Babies develop humor (exhibit joy) around the eighth month of life. When they share in our laughter they have some sense of why we are laughing. They show delight in silly games and funny sounds. Infants laugh earlier than eight months but that laughter is a learned response. Humor requires that the individual enjoying it understands the nuances that make something funny.

For some time, researchers have understood that a good sense of humor has a healthful impact on the immune system. Yet, until recently, relatively little has been known about the role humor plays in learning. Thanks to new imaging techniques, researchers are now learning more about the positive effect humor has on brain functions related to memory, alertness, and sophisticated aspects of language development, such as recognizing puns and nuances of speech.

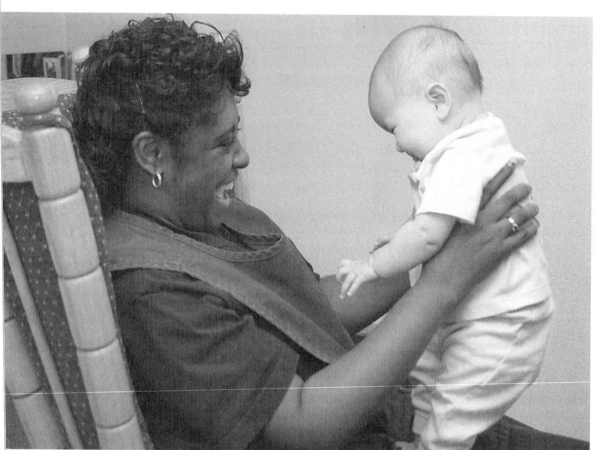

New studies are showing that humor stimulates regions of the brain known as reward centers. These reward centers release chemicals that play a vital role in the brain's pleasure and reward system. It appears that the brain feels rewarded by finding something funny. This lends credence to the idea that laughter is therapeutic—for some people it creates a natural high.

When we laugh (exhibit joy), endorphins are released into the blood stream. These act as a memory fixative, resulting in an increased ability to remember what we are experiencing. In simple terms: humor triggers emotions; emotion boosts memory. Our deepest memories are imbedded in emotion. We remember best the highs and lows of our lives.

Processing humor activates areas of the brain involved in language processing. Our ability to understand humor grows in complexity as we develop and mature. This is why humor for a two-year-old is much more simplistic than humor for an adolescent. Our understanding of humor in many cases is related to the sophistication of our language development. Because humor and language often work together, using humor exercises and strengthens our language skills (Jensen, 1995).

The development of humor begins early. Infants respond to tickle games and the game of

Peek-a-Boo during the first year of life. If humor is nurtured, it will become a habit that plays a powerful and unique role in our lives. Beyond protecting the immune system, boosting the memory, and activating and exercising language centers, it ties societies together and helps us cope with daily stress. Low stress further enhances receptivity to learning (Jensen, 1995).

Humor is an important ingredient in the daily experiences of both children and adults. The more we laugh, the more we learn, the happier we feel, and the healthier we stay.

The Caregiver's Role

You are a critical component of children's social-emotional development. One of the most important things you will do each day is to provide infants with a safe environment in which they feel both safe and content. Making sure you are there for them, taking care of their needs, and interacting with them socially will set the tone of healthy development.

Here are a few suggestions for helping children develop healthy social and emotional behaviors.

1. Respond promptly to infants' needs.
2. Handle infants gently. Avoid sudden movement. Give a warning when you are picking the baby up.
3. Talk with infants at every opportunity. Sing lullabies. Read simple books.
4. Think of ways to make infants laugh. Play simple games.
5. Be consistent! Make simple rules and abide by them always.
6. Attend to a baby's emotions by being available. Be sensitive to her cues. If she is over-stimulated, remove the source of stimulation. If she is distressed, soothe her. Teach her strategies for calming herself, such as rocking, humming, shushing, and so on.
7. Infants need to have consistency in the primary people who care for them. It is a good idea to assign each baby to a primary caregiver and to let that caregiver move up with the baby when she graduates to a new classroom.
8. Encourage infants to explore their environment. Give them freedom to climb and freedom to roam. Let them touch and feel the items that interest them. Praise them for their independence—after all, it is the ultimate goal.
9. Encourage social opportunities to play with and mix with other children. Praise children for sharing, taking turns, being gentle, and so on.
10. When an infant displays aggressive behavior, talk with her about a preferable way of handling the situation. If the infant is upset, wait until she is calm. For example, if a child hits another child you might ask, "Has anyone ever hit you? How did you feel? How do you think your friend felt when you hit her? Do you think she felt like you did?"
11. Use role playing to teach new social skills, such as saying hello to people when you

come into a room.

12. Talk about feelings and help infants understand words that describe emotions.

13. Praise infants for getting along with others and for handling difficult social situations. This will help them try these desirable behaviors again in the future.

14. Set a good example. Point out to children when you have shared things with your friends, taken turns, helped out and so on.

Experiences and Activities to Encourage a Sense of Self

Birth–18+ Months

Sense-of-Self Words to Know. Teach children vocabulary words related to sense of self. Use the words in the chart below when appropriate and as often as you can.

Angry	Eyebrows	Happy	Shoulders
Baby	Eyelashes	Head	Sister
Brother	Eyes	Hug	Smile
Chin	Family	Knees	Teacher
Clap	Feelings	Me	Teeth
Cry	Feet	Mommy	Toes
Daddy	Friends	Mouth	Wave
Dance	Glad	Nose	You
Ears	Hands	Sad	

Books About Me. Read the children books about facial expressions, senses, families, friends, and body parts. Here are a few favorites.

Baby Dance by Ann Taylor

The Baby Dances by Kathy Henderson

Baby Faces by Margaret Miller

Head to Toe by Eric Carle

How Do I Feel? by Pamela Cote

So Big (Traditional)

Toes, Ears, and Nose by Marion Dane Bauer

Look in the Mirror. Sit on the floor with one baby at a time on your lap. Talk about her facial features. *Where are your eyes? Here they are! Your eyes are a beautiful brown color. Where is your nose? My nose is here, and your nose is right here!*

Expressive Faces. Draw expressive faces on large paper plates. Make each face look a little bit different. Mount the faces on the wall. As children look at the faces, talk to them about the facial features and the facial expressions on each plate.

Birth–6 Months

These Little Hands of Mine. When you talk to the children about their hands use the poem below or some of the lines from the poem to describe the many things their hands can do.

> **These Little Hands of Mine**
> These little hands of mine
> Can do things oh so fine.
> They can reach way out,
> They can reach way up.
> They can hold a crayon,
> They can hold a cup.
> They can open and close.
> They can grab your nose.
> These little hands of mine
> Can do things oh so fine.
> They can tell what's cold,
> They can tell what's hot.
> They can tell what's sticky,
> They can tell what's not.
> They can say, "What's that?"
> They can pet the cat.
> They can give a big "Hi!"
> They can wave "goodbye."

That's Me. Ask families to provide photos of their children. Photocopy and enlarge the photo. Laminate if possible. Place each baby's picture inside her crib. When you place the baby in her crib point to her photo. Say, *That's you, Tasha. We have your picture right inside your crib.*

Foot Play. Play with baby's feet. Talk with her about her sweet little toes. Count her toes.

Kiss her toes. Recite "Baby Feet" and move baby's feet as directed.

Baby Feet by Pam Schiller
I love your baby feet. (hold baby's feet up so she can see them)
I love your little toes. (touch baby's toes)
Your little feet are sweet. (touch baby's feet to your cheek)
Let's touch them to your nose. (touch baby's feet to her nose)

Walk, walk, walk little feet. (move feet as if walking)
Run, run, run little feet. (move baby's feet faster)
Dance, dance, dance little feet. (move baby's feet in circular motion)
Sweet, sweet, sweet little feet. (touch baby's feet to your cheek)

Baby Massage. Massage the infant's hands and feet. Talk about how the lotion feels on her skin.

Little Fingers. Talk to the baby about her fingers. Tell her how strong her grasp is. Talk about the many things fingers can do. Recite "This Little Finger."

This Little Finger by Pam Schiller
This little finger holds on tight. (wiggle each finger as it is mentioned)
This little finger points just right.
This little finger helps wave "bye-bye."
This little finger wipes my eye.
This little finger holds, points, waves, and wipes.
Sweet little hands hold on tight.

Holding Hands. Place your finger in front of baby and entice her to grasp it. Hand-eye coordination begins to develop between the third and fifth months. It is greatly enhanced and refined during the seventh and eighth months when the baby is more capable of utilizing her thumb in grasping.

I Can Do It By Myself. During the first few months of life, babies need opportunities to learn strategies for calming themselves and for putting themselves to sleep. Be sensitive to needs of young infants, but remember to allow them time and opportunity to develop self-help skills. For example, instead of rocking a baby to sleep every day, comfort her and lay her down so she can master the skill of falling asleep on her own.

I Am a Separate Me. Picked up a stuffed bear or any animal. Point to the bear's eyes and then to the infant's eyes. Point to the bear's nose and then to the infant's nose. Continue for as long as she seems interested. Compare the bear's hands to her hands and to your hands. The baby won't fully understand, but the goal is to help her begin to realize that she is separate from others.

"Eyes, Ears, Nose, and Mouth." Sing "Eyes, Ears, Nose, and Mouth" to the tune of "Head, Shoulder, Knees, and Toes." Touch facial features as you sing. Try this song with older children and let the infant watch. Use a puppet or stuffed animal as a model and sing the song and point out the features of the puppet.

> **Eyes, Ears, Nose, and Mouth** adapted by Pam Schiller
> Eyes, ears, nose, and mouth—nose and mouth,
> Eyes, ears, nose, and mouth—nose and mouth,
> Two eyes, two ears, one nose, one mouth—
> Eyes, ears, nose, and mouth—nose and mouth.

6–12 Months

Eye Rhymes. Look in the mirror with the baby and recite the appropriate rhyme below or make up your own.

> **Eye Rhymes** by Pam Schiller
> You see me,
> I see you.
> Your eyes are blue. (insert the color of the baby's eyes)
> Mine are, too.
>
> Your eyes are big, and round, and brown.
> They must be the prettiest eyes in town.
>
> When I look at you, know what I see?
> Eyes as green as green can be.
>
> Blue eyes, green eyes,
> Brown eyes, hey.
> Your eyes are gray,
> And I love them that way.

Nose Rubs. Teach babies how to rub noses with you.

Bear Hugs. Teach the children how to give a "bear hug" (a tight hug). Give plenty of "bear hugs" and be sure to ask for one in return.

So Big. Hold the infant facing you on your lap. Hold her hands. Say, *How big is baby?* Answer, *Sooo big.* As you answer, open her arms wide.

Pat-a-Cake Feet. Play Pat-a-Cake (appendix page 210) using the baby's feet. Talk about her sweet little feet that will carry her anywhere she wants to go one day.

The Name Game. Say a baby's name with all its rhyming variations. For example, *Evan Evan, Bo Bevan, Banana Fana, Fo Fevan, Fee Fi, Mo Mevan, Evan.* The pattern is always the same. *David David, Bo Bavid, Banana fana, Fo Favid, Fee Fi, Mo Mavid, David.* Babies love to hear rhyming rendition of their name. Use it often.

We Can. Recite "We Can." Encourage the infants to do the actions with you. Talk about the wonderful things they can do with their bodies.

> **We Can** by Pam Schiller (suit actions to the words)
> We can jump, jump, jump,
> We can hop, hop, hop,
> We can clap, clap, clap,
> We can stop, stop, stop.
>
> We can nod our heads for yes,
> We can shake our heads for no.
> We can bend our knees a tiny bit
> And sit down slow.

Baby's Choice. Offer infants choices whenever possible. Let them choose the color of the cup they use for snack. Invite them to select which ball they prefer to play with. If you are having cookies for snack and there is a choice, let them choose which cookie they want.

Point and Do. Recite "Five Fingers on Each Hand." Encourage infants to follow your movements. Talk about the parts of their bodies. *This is your hand. It has five fingers. Here are your eyes. You use them to see.*

Five Fingers on Each Hand

I have five fingers on each hand,
Ten toes on my two feet.
Two ears, two eyes,
One nose, one mouth,
With which to sweetly speak.

My hands can clap, my feet can tap,
My eyes can clearly see.
My ears can hear,
My nose can sniff,
My mouth can say I'm me.

Expressions. Talk to infants about the expressions they make during the day. *I see you smiling. That tells me you are happy. You have a very sad expression when you cry. I can see you are unhappy.*

12–18+ Months

Brush, Brush, Brush Your Teeth. Ask families to provide a toothbrush for their child. After lunch each day, have a tooth brushing lesson. Healthy habits begin early. Use the "Tooth Brushing Song" to add some fun to the activity.

> **Tooth Brushing Song** by Pam Schiller (Tune: Here We Go 'Round the Mulberry Bush)
> This is the way we brush our teeth,
> Brush our teeth, brush our teeth.
> This is the way we brush our teeth,
> Every day and night.
>
> We move the brush up and down,
> Up and down, up and down.
> We move the brush up and down
> Every time we brush.

Squeaky Clean. Teach the infants to wash their faces. Sing "This Is the Way We Wash Our Face" as you wash.

> **This Is the Way Wash Our Face** by Pam Schiller (Tune: Here We Go 'Round the Mulberry Bush)
> This is the way we wash our face,
> Scrub our cheeks, scrub our ears.
> This is the way we wash our face,
> Until we're squeaky clean.

I Can, Can You? Say the rhyme below with the infants. Help younger infants with the movements.

> **I Can, Can You?** by Pam Schiller
> I can put my hands up high. Can you?
> I can stick out my tongue. Can you?
> I can nod my head. Can you?
> I can kiss my toe. Can you?
> I can pull on my ear. Can you?
> I can touch my nose. Can you?
> I can give myself a great big hug. Can you?
> And if I give my hug to you, will you give yours to me?

A Hug for Me. Teach the infants how to hug themselves, give a "high five," and a "thumbs up." Use these signs to celebrate their accomplishments.

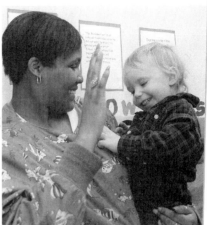

Hand Washing. Talk with children about proper hand-washing techniques while they are washing their hands. Talk about using soap correctly and putting it back where it belongs when they are finished. Point out the need to wash their between fingers and how to dry their hands when they are finished. Use the "Hand Washing Song" below to add to the fun.

Hand Washing Song by Pam Schiller (Tune: The Farmer in the Dell)
It's time to wash our hands.
It's time to wash our hands.
Hi ho, hooray for hands,
It's time to wash our hands.

Let's turn the water on.
Let's turn the water on.
Hi, ho, hooray for hands,
It's time to wash our hands.

Now add a little soap.
Now add a little soap.
Hi, ho, hooray for hands,
It's time to wash our hands.

Don't forget your fingers.
Don't forget your fingers.
Hi, ho, hooray for hands,
It's time to wash our hands.

We dry our hands at last.
We dry our hands at last.
Hi, ho, hooray for hands,
We washed and dried our hands.

Do You Know Your Name! Focus on one child. Call her name many times throughout the day. Does she seem to recognize her name when she hears it? Does she turn to you?

Face Puzzles. Ask families for photos of their child. Make face puzzles by enlarging the photo, mounting it on poster board, and cutting it into puzzle pieces. Start with simple puzzles cut with simple lines and in no more than three pieces. Make puzzles increasingly more complex by cutting them into more pieces.

Face Puppets. Draw a happy face and a sad face on 6" paper plates. Tape or glue the plates to plastic straws to make puppets. Use the puppets playfully to demonstrate happy and sad facial expressions. Encourage infants to smile. Encourage them to show you a frowning face.

Where Are Your Ears? Ask the infant to point to her ears, eyes, mouth, and nose. Ask her to point to the same facial features on your face. Here is a rhyme you can share with her. You may want to break it into parts and do one verse at a time.

Here Are My Ears (suit actions to words)
Here are my ears,
Here is my nose.
Here are my fingers,
Here are my toes.

Here are my eyes,
Both open wide.
Here is my mouth,
With white teeth inside.

Here is my tongue,
That helps me speak.
Here is my chin,
And here are my cheeks.

Here are my hands,
That help me play.
Here are my feet,
For walking today.

Feelings Blocks. Make a set of Feelings Blocks (appendix page 228). Encourage the children to build with the blocks. As they are building, talk with them about the illustrations on each block. Ask one child to find a happy face. *This face looks angry. Does it look angry to you?*

What Face Is This? Sit in front of a mirror with infants and make faces. Have children show you a sad face, a happy face, and a really sad face.

Body Talk. Say the rhyme "My Body Talks" with the infants. Discuss all the ways we use our body to communicate.

> **My Body Talks** by Pam Schiller
> When I want to say, "Hello," I wave my hand.
> When I want to say, "No," I shake my head from side to side.
> When I want to say, "Yes," I nod my head up and down.
> When I want to say, "Good job," I stick up my thumb.
> When I want to say, "I disagree," I turn my thumb down.
> When I want to celebrate a success, I clap my hands.
> When I want to say, "Enough," or "Stop," I hold my hand out.
> When I want to say, "Come here," I wave my hand toward me.
> When I want to say, "Goodbye," I wave my hand or blow you a kiss.
> When I want to say, "I love you," I wrap my arms around you and squeeze.

I Like Me. Teach babies to give themselves a hug by crossing their arms across their chest and squeezing.

Friends Are Wonderful. Copy, laminate, and put a magnet on the back of pictures of the infants in the classroom. Give them the pictures and a magnetic board or cookie sheet. Sit with children as they play. **Safety Note:** Be sure they do not put the magnets in their mouths. Talk to them about how much fun friends add to our lives.

You Are Special. Sing songs to children that reinforce their sense of feeling special. Older children will be able to sing along with you. Younger ones will listen and maybe even hum along.

> **I Am Special** by Pam Schiller (Tune: Where Is Thumbkin?)
> I am special, I am special.
> Yes, I am. Yes, I am.
> Special to my mommy,
> Special to my daddy,
> Special, special me.
> Special, special me.

Emotional Expressions. Talk with infants during the day about emotions they are expressing. *I can tell you are feeling sad right now. You are angry. It is taking too long to get your food ready. Look at that big smile. You are really happy.*

Build a Face. Cut felt into parts of the face—eyes, ears, mouths, noses, and hair. Provide a flannel board and encourage babies to build a face.

Head, Shoulder, Knees, and Toes. Sing "Head, Shoulders, Knees, and Toes." Who can do the movements? Help those who aren't able to do the movements.

> **Head, Shoulders, Knees, and Toes** (touch body parts as they are mentioned
>   in the song)
> Head, shoulders, knees, and toes,
> Knees and toes.
> Head, shoulders, knees, and toes,
> Knees and toes.
> Eyes and ears and mouth and nose.
> Head, shoulders, knees, and toes,
> Knees and toes.

18+ Months

Bathe the Baby. Provide a rubber doll and all the necessary accessories to bathe and diaper it, such as a tub of water, towel, lotion, comb, towel, diaper, and so on. Talk with the infant about the steps in bathing. Ask her about her bath time. You may want to sing "Evan's Tub Tune" as you help children bathe the baby.

> **Evan's Tub Time** by Richele Bartkowiak (Tune: Rock-a-Bye Baby)
> Splishin' and a splashin'
> In the bathtub.
> When we take a bath
> We clean and we scrub.
> With our washcloth
> And a little shampoo.
> And when it's all over
> We smell good as new.
>
> Splishin' and a splashin'
> That's what we do.
> Don't forget Ducky,
> He likes it too.
> Watchin' the bubbles
> Dance in the tub.
> Oh how we love bath time
> Rub-a-dub-dub!

Me Puzzles. Make Me Puzzles (appendix page 231) for older children. Encourage them to work the puzzles. Talk with them about their facial features.

Sing a Song of Friendship. Teach the children "The Friendship Song." Ask one infant to name a friend. Encourage this child to sing the song to her friend. For those children who are not yet able to sing the song, sing it for them.

> **The Friendship Song** (Tune: Do You Know the Muffin Man?)
> Do you know you are my friend,
> You are my friend, you are my friend?
> Do you know you are my friend?
> I like to play with you.

Playdough Faces. Show the children how to make a face out of playdough. Make a pancake for the face. Add large buttons, large wiggle eyes, pieces of felt, pipe cleaners and other materials to create facial features. If you use a pipe cleaner for the mouth, show the children how to turn it upside down to make a frown. **Safety Note:** Supervise closely so children do not put objects in their mouths.

Experiences and Activities to Build Trust

Birth–18+ Months

Trust Words to Know. Teach children vocabulary words and phrases related to trust. Use the words and phrases in the chart below when appropriate and as often as you can.

Care	Here	Love	Special
Coming	Hug	Needs	You
Concern	I'm here	Okay	
Count on me	Important	Smile	
Depend	Like	Snuggle	

Books About Trust. Read books about trust. Here are a few favorites:

Counting Kisses: A Kiss and Read Book by Karen Katz
Guess How Much I Love You? by Sam McBratney
Hug by Jez Alborough
Where Is Baby's Mommy? by Karen Katz

My Time. Set aside a special time each day for each baby. Spend a few minutes with each child and make sure that that time belongs only to her. Talk with her, rock her, look at her with eyes that communicate how wonderful and unique she is. This will take some effort and organization but it is possible and it goes a long way toward building rapport and trust.

It's in the Voice. Use calm and loving voices with infants. Loud voices, even when directed at others, are upsetting to them. Always a voice that is firm but not frightening.

Rock Me, Hug Me. Babies need to feel the comfort of touch. Rocking, hugging, and cuddling are basic needs for infants. When you don't have time for more elaborate forms of touching, use a love pat or a gentle squeeze.

I Can Do Anything You Can Do! Mirror the noises and movements that babies make. We may not be able to understand them but we can connect with them through imitation. This shows acceptance and it encourages them to continue to practice their sounds and movements.

My Family. Ask families to provide pictures of each family member. Display the photos at the infants' eye level (consider your crawlers) on the wall. Cover them with plastic sheeting or Plexiglas. When children start missing mommy or daddy take them to the display to see their family members.

Familiar Smells. Encourage family members to leave something with you that has their scent on it, for example, a shirt, scarf, or pillowcase. Place the item in the crib with the baby during naptime.

Story Time Buddies. Find time to read to infants individually as often as possible. Take one child aside. Sit in a comfortable place and read a book. Story time offers a great opportunity for cuddling and feeling special.

Sleeping Habits. Infants need to learn to put themselves to sleep without relying on "crutches." Rocking and patting babies to sleep interferes with their ability to master self-regulating behavior. Rock them almost to sleep and then lay them down and let them finish the task.

Lotion Rub. Rub baby lotion all over the infant's body before nap or after bath time. Talk about how nice the lotion feels and how much you love doing things that make her comfortable and happy. Discuss the scent of the lotion. Before naptime you may want to use a chamomile and lavender scent as it creates a sense of calm.

Bath Time Fun. If you bathe infants, make bath time fun. Use only soaps and shampoos that are gentle and will not burn their eyes. Add bath time toys and change the toys over time to create a new discovery. A good song for bath time is Evan's Tub Time (appendix page 188). Here is an after-bath poem.

> **After My Bath** by Pam Schiller
> After my bath I try, try, try
> To rub with a towel till I'm dry, dry, dry.
> Hands to dry, and fingers and toes,
> And two wet legs and a shiny nose.
> Just think how much less time it'd take,
> If I were a dog and could shake, shake, shake!

Morning Greetings. Greet every child every day in a special way. You can give each one a hug, sing a little song, or say a little rhyme. Children like the predictability of your greeting. Greeting time is one of the times during the day that familiar routines are welcome. Greetings that you use with children provide a model for greetings they will someday use with friends and family.

> **Hello, Friends**
> Hello, good friend.
> Hello, good friend.
> How are you, Austin?

Morning Greeting

Madison, Madison,

Howdy-do.

Hello. Good day.

How are you?

Hello (Tune: Are You Sleeping?)

Hello, Maria,

Hello, Maria.

How are you?

How are you?

I'm so glad to see you.

I'm so glad to see you.

Let's go play.

Let's go play.

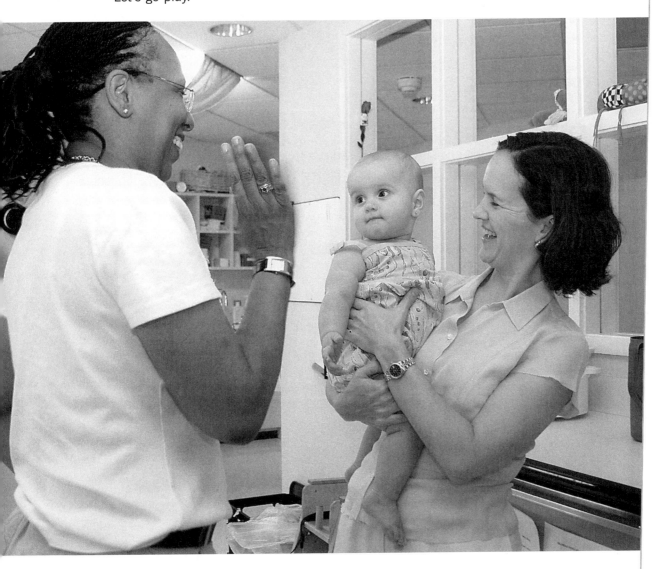

Stress Busters. Make a list of strategies you can use to help babies reduce their anxiety and calm themselves. Your list might include rocking, walking, humming, "shushing," providing a special toy or blanket, or looking out a window. Place the list in a convenient place so you can refer to it when needed. As you use the various strategies, verbalize them to the child. Someday she will have to find her own strategies to reduce her anxiety.

Sing a Song of Care. When a baby is crying, try singing to make her less fussy. Try singing the song below.

> **I'm Here to Take Care of You** adapted by Pam Schiller (Tune: Oh, Dear, What Can the Matter Be?)
> Oh, dear, what can the matter be?
> Oh, dear, what can the matter be?
> Oh, dear, what can the matter be?
> I think you are calling me.
>
> I'm here to take care of you, dear.
> I'm here to take care of you, dear.
> I'm here to take care of you, dear.
> Let's wipe away that tear.

Rock-a-Bye Baby. Sing lullabies to babies when naptime approaches. All infants become calm to the rhythm of a good lullaby. Use the ones below or find others in the appendix on pages 186–198.

> **Bye Baby Bunting**
> Bye baby bunting
> Daddy's gone a'hunting
> Mummy's gone a'milking
> Sister's gone a'silking
> Brother's gone to buy a skin
> To wrap the baby bunting in.
>
> **Tell Me Why**
> Tell me why the stars do shine,
> Tell me why the ivy twines,
> Tell me why the skies are blue,
> And I will tell you just why I love you.

Butterfly Kisses. Share "Butterfly Kisses" (eyelash flutters on the cheek) with babies on a regular basis.

Baby Transitions. Notify a child when you are going to pick her up, change her diaper, place her in her feeding chair, or any other movement. This works just as transitions do with older children. Your words, even though she may not understand them yet, signal that there is going to be a change.

Birth–6 Months

I'm Coming. Talk to the infant from a distance when she is a little bit fussy. Let her know that you are close by. Sometimes, infants just need to know you are near. It is important for infants to learn to calm themselves. However, if the fussing doesn't stop, go to the infant and pick her up.

I'm Here. When babies are not just fussing, but really crying, go to them immediately. There is no such thing as spoiling a baby. If you are busy with another child, let the crying baby know that you are coming by calling their name and assuring them you are on your way.

You and Me. Make a special time every day for every baby. This should not be feeding time or naptime, but a time that you can simply hold them and talk to them. Play games with them. Sing songs. Read books. Blow bubbles.

Hum and Sway. When babies are fussy, hold them close, hum softly, and sway gently from side to side.

Tummy to Tummy. Lie on the floor with a baby on your tummy and talk to her. She will lift her head to listen. Older infants may even babble and coo along with you.

Swaddling. Wrapping an infant snugly often helps to keep her calm. Place the baby diagonally on a receiving blanket. Pull one side of the blanket across her body. Pull the bottom corner up and then pull the other side of the blanket snugly around her. Babies feel more secure when their bodies are wrapped in a blanket. Getting used to the freedom that comes with being outside the womb takes a little time.

Eye-to-Eye Connections. During the first few months of life, babies connect with others by making eye contact. At first they aren't able to hold their gaze for long, but with practice and time, the length of the time they can hold contact increases. Make eye contact with a baby and enjoy the closeness that is a natural part of looking into the eyes of someone who thinks you are wonderful.

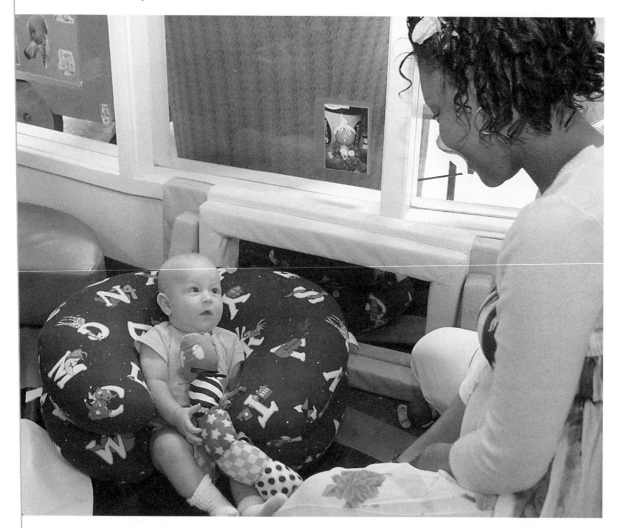

A New Perspective. When a baby is lying on the floor, position yourself at her head and lean over her so that she is looking at you upside down. Talk to her about what she sees.

Beach Ball Ride. Blow up a large inflatable ball. Sit in a carpeted area of the room with a baby. Place her on the ball on her stomach and gently roll the ball forward and backward.

Dance With Me, Baby. Hold a child on your shoulders and dance around the room. Play interesting music, samba, polka, and waltz tunes. Don't forget to thank your partner for the dance.

I'm Picking You Up. Warn an infant before you pick her up by saying *Ups-a-Daisy*. You will find that pretty soon *Ups-a-Daisy* brings a smile to her face—her way of granting permission and even expressing joy.

Elephant Trunk Swing. Hold an infant in your arms, bend at the waist, and gently sway back and forth. Talk with her about your movements.

Cat Roll. Lie on your back with the baby lying on your chest. Roll from side to side while holding her in place. Talk with her about her ride.

Blanket Rides. Lay a large towel or small blanket on the floor and place the infant on the blanket. Slowly and carefully pull her around the room. Talk about the things you see. Talk about how she is balancing.

Gentle Reminders. When an infant stops sucking her bottle before it is empty, try gently rubbing your finger on her cheek or under her chin to get her drinking again.

Sleepy Time Talk. When you put an infant in her crib for naptime, stay beside the crib and talk to her for a minute or two. Rub her tummy. Tell her to have sweet dreams. Stroke her cheek. Tell her you'll see her when she wakes.

A Cushioned Fall. When babies are learning to sit up but are still a little bit wobbly, sit them inside a "Boppy™" or place an inflatable inner tube around their waists. That way, if they fall over they have a cushioned landing.

6–12 Months

Your Hands, My Hands. Compare your hands to the baby's hands. *Whose hands are larger? Who has the smallest hands? How many fingers are on your hand? How many fingers are on my hands?* Tell baby how sweet her hands are.

Dancing Partners. Play some dance music and invite walkers to hold your hands and dance to the music. Take the "not yet walkers" in your arms and dance them around the room.

Sweet Nothings. Whisper sweet words to the infant. She will love the change from your normal voice and will enjoy the closeness that comes from sharing a whisper.

I'm Here for You. As you hold the infant, say the poem "We're Here for Each Other." Think about the words of the poem. They hold a message for both of you.

> **We're Here for Each Other** by Pam Schiller
> Every day I'm here for you.
> I give you a smile for every coo.
> I get your bottle and keep you dry.
> I hold you close when you cry.
>
> Every day you're here for me.
> When I'm blue you seem to see.
> You smile and coo as if to say,
> "I'm here to cheer you through the day."

Rocker Time. Each day, spend time rocking the infants. Rocking gives you some special time with infants and also aids their coordination and balance. Rocking stimulates the vestibular system, which determines both balance and coordination.

Truck Rides. Lie on your back on the floor and invite an infant to straddle your tummy for a bumpy truck ride. Bounce up and down and make a truck sound.

Horsie Rides. Lie on your back on a carpeted area of the floor. Lift your legs and bend your knees. Invite a child to sit on your ankles and lean on your shins. Hold her hand and bounce your legs for a pony ride. You might want to hum the "William Tell Overture."

Comfort Talk. Talk to the baby to let her know you are aware she needs you. For example, say, *I'm coming* or *Just a minute*. Perhaps pat her on the head or call her name. There are many ways of acknowledging a baby's cry for help.

12–18+ Months

Safety First. Talk to the infants about your classroom. Tell them that the classroom is a safe place. Tell them that while they are with you, you will keep them safe. Feeling safe precedes the ability to learn. To maximize learning, children must first feel comfortable and safe.

Lunch Time Date. Make it a point to have lunch with a baby on a day when it works well. Perhaps there is a day when a baby's schedule is off a little and she eats a little earlier or later than her friends or a day when you have enough extra hands to enable you to create a special time for you and her. Babies between 12–18 months are finger-food lovers so take advantage of this opportunity to have your hands free to feed yourself. She will love having company for lunch.

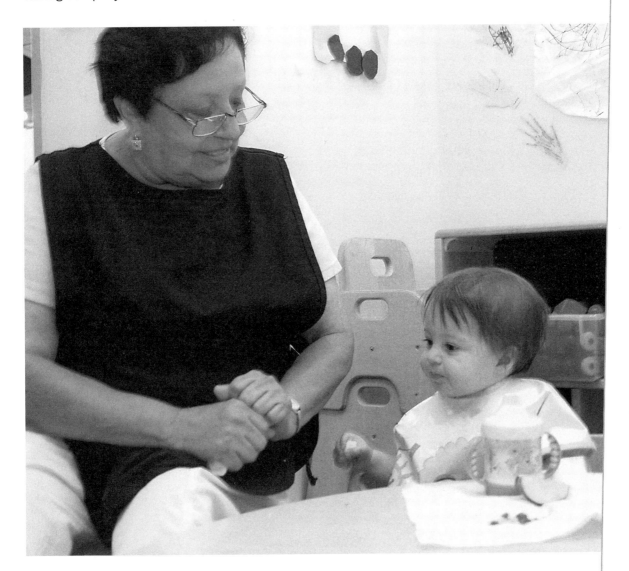

I Like You. Tell babies often how much you like them. Tell them about the things that make them special and uniquely different.

A "One-Rule" Rule. Try to have just one rule for the classroom. For example, *You can do anything you like in our classroom as long as you don't hurt yourself or anyone else.* When you think about it, that pretty much covers everything. It is like the Golden Rule. Remind children of the rule when necessary. Be firm, fair, and consistent. Consistency builds trust.

Love Songs. Sing love songs to babies, such as "Skidamarink" below and "Tell Me Why" (appendix page 196). Try others that you like such as "Oh, Do You Know I Love You So," "You Are My Sunshine," and "I Love You a Bushel and a Peck."

Skidamarink

Skidamarink a dink a dink,
Skidamarink a doo,
I love you.
Skidamarink a dink a dink,
Skidamarink a doo,
I love you.

I love you in the morning
And in the afternoon,
I love you in the evening
And underneath the moon;
Oh, Skidamarink a dink a dink,
Skidamarink a doo,
I love you!

Saying Goodbye. Help babies say goodbye easily to family members in the morning. Work with family members to quickly make their departure, and be clear with their baby about their love and about their return. Following is a reminder to post on the wall. It will help family members remember the routine.

Saying Goodbye

1. Put my things in my cubby.
2. Tell me you love me.
3. Give me a hug.
4. Tell me you'll be back soon.

When family members are consistent and clear, infants will learn to say goodbye, and they will become confident that someone will return for them.

Accentuate the Positive. Focus on the positive. The more positive your comments and expectations, the more positive children's attitudes and behaviors will be. Use positive words, such as *good job*, *well done*, *terrific*, *super*, and *great* and supporting gestures, such as thumbs up, high-five, and an "okay" sign.

Taking Turns. When working with babies on taking turns, use an egg timer or kitchen timer to divide time evenly between the two children who want to share a riding toy or a favorite toy. Fairness builds trust and staying fair is not easy when you are holding on to so many strings. A timer takes the pressure off you.

Quick Response. Getting to a fussy baby as quickly as possible is imperative. When infants are fussy, soothe them with your voice as you are approaching them. Let them know that you hear their cry and that you are coming. If you tend to baby quickly, he is less likely to be demanding of your attention. Remember you cannot spoil a baby (birth to 18 months).

It's a Date. Make a point of planning a special time for each baby every day. Read a book together, take a stroll, talk, rock, sing, play a game. It is important that babies know that they don't have to share you all the time.

Tender Hands. Babies are sensitive to your touch. If you touch them with frustration or anger they feel it right away. Only pick up a baby with loving and gentle hands. If you are stressed, ask someone to take care of the baby until you calm down. Tension breeds tension, and a room full of tense babies is not a place anyone wants to be.

18+ Months

Little Helpers. Older infants love to help. Let them know you trust them to help you when possible. Perhaps they can fetch a diaper or bring a toy to calm another child.

Routines Build Trust. Keep routines as consistent as possible for children. Routines are the framework of their existence. Routines are like watches to babies. It lets them know where they are in time. It provides predictability. Talk with a baby about routines and in terms of routines. *We have story time after lunch. We have snack after naptime.*

Consistency. Hold fast to consistency. If it is not safe for Kira to crawl under the table then it is not safe for any other child to do so. If it is not safe to crawl under the table on Monday then it is not safe on Tuesday. Make sure your rules are what you want them to be and that they work. Then make sure they are the same for all children all the time.

Piggyback Rides. Take babies on piggyback rides. Do they trust you enough to hang on to your back? Of course, once they decide they do, you may wish you never started this activity!

Experiences and Activities to Develop Impulse Control

15–18+ Months

Self-Control Words to Know. Teach children vocabulary words related to self-control. Use the words and phrases in the chart below when appropriate.

Be patient	No	Share	Wrong
Choice	Others	Smart	Yes
Enough	Responsible	Stop	You're next
Less	Right	Think	
More	Rules	Turn	

Books About Boundaries. Read books about boundaries and manners. Here are some favorites:

Counting Kisses: A Kiss and Read Book by Karen Katz
Excuse Me: A Little Book on Manners by Karen Katz
No Biting by Sandra Boynton

Set Boundaries. Develop a set of simple rules and hold to them firmly. Infants need to know what is acceptable and what is not acceptable. They need to understand that crying doesn't change a rule and crying doesn't change your answer to their denied request. Be consistent above all else.

Sign Language Help. Teach the children to use American Sign Language signs that deal with self-control (appendix pages 247–249). Communication enables children to be more self-regulated.

Classroom Community Rituals. Develop several different strategies for helping children understand that they are a community of learners and are each responsible for making sure that everyone in the group is safe and secure. Verbally stating that everyone is safe and secure is one way of helping children understand their connection to one another. You may also want to create a visual reminder by gluing every child's photo to a heart-shaped piece of poster board and displaying it in a prominent place in the classroom. For more suggestions on creating a safe and secure environment, see *I Love You Rituals* by Becky Bailey (appendix page 253).

Offer Choices. Whenever possible, offer choices to babies. Choices give everyone a sense of some control. As babies approach the two-year-old mark they are driven to determine that they have some control over their life.

Notice Me. Babies will go to great extremes in trying to get your attention—especially in a group situation. Reinforce appropriate methods and redirect inappropriate methods. Infants may tug hard at your pants leg, cry, scream, and even hit you. Show them a better way to get your attention, such as a gentle pat on your leg.

Resolving Conflicts. Talk with infants about their disputes even though you know that they don't yet understand exactly what you are saying. For example, if two children both want the same riding toy, say, *Tiffany, it is Phil's turn to ride. You can have the truck when Phil finishes. Phil, please let Tiffany know when you are finished.* This type of rational problem solving will soon catch on. Children will learn to negotiate their own conditions.

Timers. Use timers to signal the end of play, to time each child's turn on a riding toy, and to warn babies that clean-up time is approaching. Timers are visible and audible signs that babies come to understand.

Focus. Make sure that infants are paying attention when you are explaining boundaries and/or rules. Hold them by the shoulders. Have them look you in the eyes (if culturally acceptable). Speak clearly and distinctly and keep it short. If the infant is verbal, ask her to repeat the information back to you.

Watch for Signs. Pay attention to babies as they play. When they become tired, it is difficult for them to stay in control. When you notice that children are becoming tired, begin to prepare for a rest. Children don't follow our schedules—we adjust to their schedules. If it means eating early and going down for a nap before the scheduled time, do it.

Staying Calm. Keep chamomile hand lotion by the hand-washing sink. Use chamomile and lavender soap for hand washing. Chamomile is a calming scent. Staying calm helps when infants are learning to control their emotions and feelings.

Smooth Transitions. Make sure that children know when you are getting ready to change activities. Give them a warning in advance and clearly communicate what is expected. This will help infants self-regulate their reactions to the change. Use music, lights on and off, bells, timers, or any other clear signal that change is coming.

Transition Songs. Use songs to help children develop good habits and to assist them in making smooth transitions. Here are a couple of songs and chants that work well with cleanup time and with preparing to sit quietly.

> **Cleanup Time** (Tune: Do You Know the Muffin Man?)
> Oh, can you put the toys away,
> Toys away, toys away?
> Oh, can you put the toys away?
> It's time to end our play.
>
> **Be Very Quiet**
> Shhh—be very quiet,
> Shhh—be very still.
> Fold your busy little hands,
> Close your sleepy little eyes.
> Shhh—be very quiet.

No Time Out. "Time out" is not acceptable in the infant classroom. Use distraction, ignoring, if possible, and redirection. All of these strategies are far more suitable for babies.

Mean What You Say. Think before giving children answers to their request. Once you have answered you must stick to what you have said. So, be sure to mean what you say and say what you mean.

Finish What You Start.
Encourage children to finish what they start. This is a habit that will serve them all of their lives and its development starts now. When they start a puzzle, help them finish it. When they take out the blocks, help them build something before they decide to move on. And before they move on, show them how to put the blocks away. Part of controlling impulses includes learning not to "flit."

A Place for Things. Keep toys in the classroom organized. It is important to have plenty of toys, but too many toys are over-stimulating. When children are over-stimulated they become unfocused and possibly out of control. Rotate the toys for variety but remember to limit the number of toys available at any one time. Think about how you feel when you are in a place that is cluttered and remember that it takes less to create clutter for children than it does for you.

"Setting rules and being consistent in following the rules will help infants identify boundaries and wire behaviors that are within the limits of the boundaries."

Experiences and Activities to Enhance Social Interactions

Birth–18+ Months

Social Interaction Words to Know. Teach children vocabulary words and phrases related to social interactions. Use the words and phrases in the chart below when appropriate and as often as you can.

Buddy	Me	Play	Thank you
Fair	Mine	Please	Turns
Friend	Nice	Share	Use
Kind	Ours	Speak	Words
Laugh	Partner	Talk	Yours
May I			

Books About Friends. Read books about friends and family. Here are some favorites:

Baby Faces by Dorling Kindersley Publishing
Where Is Baby's Mommy? by Karen Katz

Baby Cues. Take cues from babies. Babies do an incredibly effective job of self-regulating. They will let you know when they are hungry, sleepy, or ready for interaction. They will also let you know when they are finished eating, want to be alone, or need comfort.

Family Photos. Display photos of each baby's family in a prominent place in the classroom or place them in plastic resealable bags and make a Family Photo Album. One great way to display photos is to place them on the floor and cover them with a thin sheet of Plexiglas that is taped securely to the floor.

Me Photos. Ask families to provide photos of their child. Display photos of children in the diaper-changing area of the room.

Please and Thank You. Teach babies to say *please* and *thank you*. Use these words when you speak to them and encourage them to use the words with you and others. When infants begin to speak, insert the words where they belong in their speech. If you use sign language in the classroom, make *please* and *thank you* two of the first words you teach.

Peek-a-Boo Photo. Make a Peek-a-Boo Photo (appendix page 232) and use it to play Peek-a-Boo and other games with babies. A puppet can also talk to babies.

Birth–6 Months

Special Time Meals. Make feeding time a special time. Get comfortable when feeding babies. Relax. Sing quietly or talk with infants while they eat.

Baby Buddies. Place babies on the floor facing each other. Encourage the pairs to observe each other. Say, *Look at Ian's pretty eyes. Doesn't Richele have a cute little nose?*

Let's Practice Smiling. You are infants' social focal point. Work with them on learning to smile. A smile is an invitation to connect socially. Generally, babies learn to smile between six and eight weeks. They learn to smile by watching people smile at them. Smile often throughout the day. Babies will smile back, and they will also develop the habit of smiling. Sing a song about smiling, such as the one on the next page.

Smile at Me by Pam Schiller (Tune: Row, Row, Row Your Boat)
Smile, smile, smile at me,
And I will smile at you.
Every time you give a smile
It always turns to two.

Eye to Eye. Make and maintain eye contact with a baby for as long as she is able to stay focused. Connecting with babies' eyes is one of the first steps in bonding and one of the first ways that a baby begins to gain information about her world. You will notice that babies get better and better at being able to hold their focus. It is an extremely difficult task, so be sure to praise baby for her effort.

Baby Faces. Between the fifth and sixth month, babies develop depth perception and are better able to discriminate pictures in books. Show babies one of the many books that focus on baby faces. Babies love to look at faces.

Company. Ask families to provide pictures of their babies. Copy and enlarge the photos. Place a few photos inside each baby's crib. They will learn to recognize the familiar faces in the classroom.

Seesaw. Sit on the floor and bend your knees. Sit the infant on your feet and hold her hands. Say, "Seesaw, Millie McGraw."

Seesaw, Millie McGraw adapted by Pam Schiller
Seesaw, Millie McGraw,
Rocking slow,
Back and forth we go,
Seesaw, Millie McGraw.

Your Turn, My Turn. Practice the social interaction and give and take of "you coo, I smile, you smile, I coo." This is the predecessor to "you coo, I coo."

You Coo, I Coo. When babies become well established "cooers," begin to work on the "your turn, my turn" aspect of conversation. When they stop cooing you start talking. Stop after a few words and look at them expectantly. Encourage them to take their turn. *It's your turn. Come on.*

Rocking Time. Rock babies and recite the chant "Rocking To and Fro." You are the center of baby's social world. Talk to the baby about how special she is and how much you love her.

Rocking To and Fro by Pam Schiller
Rocking, rocking,
Rocking to and fro.
Rocking, rocking
Back and forth we go.

Baby Talk. While you are changing baby's diaper, have older infants help by talking to the baby. Babies are fascinated by their older counterparts.

6–12 Months

Puppet Play. Use a puppet to play with children. Have the puppet sing a song to them. Show the baby how the puppet can bow and clap for herself when she finishes her song.

Bumblebee Buzz. Play Bumblebee with infants. "Fly" your pointer finger through the air like a bumblebee. Make a buzzing sound as you move. After a few seconds, use your pointer finger to tickle baby under the chin, under the arm, or lightly on the tummy. Bumblebee is a visual tracking game. Watch for baby to follow your finger with her eyes.

Hey, Look It Over! When spoon-feeding an infant, let her see the food on the spoon. Hold the spoon 10"–12" away from her face. No one likes to have something they can't see shoved into their face. Wait for the baby to show signs of readiness, such as parting her lips or opening her mouth. Don't rush feeding. Name the food as you put it into her mouth.

Little Mouse. Play "Little Mouse" with babies.

> **Little Mouse**
> Walk little mouse, walk little mouse. (walk fingers up baby's arm)
> Hide little mouse, hide little mouse. (hide fingers under baby's arm)
> Here comes the cat! (be still, look around)
> Run little mouse, run little mouse! (walk fingers quickly back down baby's arm)

Crawling Hide and Seek. Crawl alongside a baby and then crawl ahead and hide behind a locker or a wall. Stick your head out and say, *Hi,* as baby crawls past.

Rolling Photo Album. Ask families to provide photos of their infant and of themselves. Follow the directions for making Family Roll-Overs (appendix page 227). Encourage the infants to pay attention to the photos on the box as they roll it across the floor. Do they recognize friends? Do they recognize family members? Can they find their own photo?

Lunch Buddies. At lunchtime, arrange feeding trays so that each baby has a buddy to look at while eating.

Side by Side. Make Me and My Friend Photos (appendix page 231) for infants. Talk with them about their friend. Let them keep their photos close by as they play.

Friendship Dance. Play some dance music and dance with two children at the same time. Tell little dancers that you are a dancing troupe.

Chew Your Food. Talk with babies as they eat their food. Discuss the texture, color, and taste of the food. Encourage them to take small bites and to chew their food well. Here is a song you may want to sing as they eat. Talk about the word *chew*.

> **Chew, Chew, Chew Your Food** by Pam Schiller (Tune: Row, Row, Row Your Boat)
> Chew, chew, chew your food
> A little at a time.
> Chew it slow, chew it good,
> Chew it to this rhyme.

Beautiful Mommy. Sing to a baby about her family members. Here is a song about mommy and a poem about families. A baby's family is her first social circle.

Beautiful Mommy (Tune: K-K-K Katie)
M-m-m-mommy, beautiful mommy
I love you more and more and more and more.
M-m-m-mommy, beautiful mommy,
You're the only m-m-m-mommy I adore.

My Family
Mommy and I dance and sing.
Daddy and I laugh and play.
Mommy, Daddy, and I
Dance and sing,
Laugh and play,
Kiss and hug,
A zillion times a day!

Where's Michaela? While sitting with babies ask them to find friends in the classroom. *Where's Nadia? Where's Sky?* If the baby doesn't point or look at the children in question, give her a hint. *Is that Michaela close to the door?* Include caregivers.

12–18+ Months

Class Album. Ask families to provide photos of their infant. Place the photos in a Plastic Bag Book (page 232). Encourage the children to look through the album. Do they recognize their friends? Can they find their picture?

Friend Puppets. Ask families for a photo of their child. Make Friend Puppets (appendix page 228). Encourage the children to play with the Friend Puppets. Ask them to match puppets to friends. Ask "talkers" to name the puppets.

Do for Others. Encourage infants to help each other. When someone gets hurt, ask the other children what might be done to make her feel better. When a child needs assistance and the need is something an older child can help with, such as reaching a toy or finding a special block, encourage the older child to help.

Family-Style Lunch. When children are around 15 months old, eat together as a family. Make lunchtime a special family time. Caregivers and children are a family. Infants will eat more slowly and will be more likely to experiment with eating new foods when lunchtime becomes a social experience. This is also a good time to model manners.

Finger Delights. Serve finger foods such as sliced bananas, dried cereal, cooked sausages, and fish sticks. Occasionally, not using a spoon makes eating so much easier.

THE COMPLETE RESOURCE BOOK FOR INFANTS

The More We Get Together. Sing "The More We Get Together" with the children. Name each child in the group and remind the children that they are classroom friends. Talk with older children about friends. If children have special friends that they are particularly fond of, mention the pairs.

> ### The More We Get Together
> The more we get together,
> Together, together,
> The more we get together,
> The happier are we.

Rub-a-Dub-Dub. Invite three little explorers to get inside a large cardboard box or inside a large laundry basket. Recite the modified "Rub-a-Dub-Dub" rhyme as you interact with babies.

> ### Rub-a-Dub-Dub
> Rub-a-dub-dub, (gently rock box or basket)
> Three babes in a tub.
> And who do you think they be?
> Gabrielle, Madison, and Austin, (insert names of babies)
> Turn them around all three. (turn the box or basket)

Hello and Goodbye. Teach infants ways to say "hello" and "goodbye" to each other. They can wave, hug, speak, or nod.

Beach Ball Roll. Blow up a small, inflatable ball. Show babies how to roll it back and forth to each other.

Friend Search. Call children's names and ask the other children to find her. *Where's Madison? Where's Ian? Can you find Quinn?* Encourage the children to point to their friends when the names are called.

Older Friends. Invite children from an older class to come for a visit during playtime. Encourage them to play with babies. Give them suggestions of things they can play that babies will enjoy, such as Peek-a-Boo or Pat-a-Cake.

Picnic Fun. Plan an old-fashioned picnic. Make it a cooperative effort. On a nice spring day, pack lunches and take the infants outdoors to eat. Let older infants help you pack. Let them help carry items outdoors. Take some balls outdoors and encourage the infants to play together.

It Takes Two. Involve children in games that take two people to play, such as rolling a ball or a truck back and forth or creating a breeze by holding the ends of a pillowcase and quickly raising and lowering it.

Group Games. Play "London Bridge Is Falling Down" (appendix page 217), "Ring Around the Rosy" (appendix page 218), or other group games (see appendix pages 217–18) with babies.

Magnetic Friends. Place friends' photos in magnetic picture holders. Give the photos to babies along with a large cookie sheet. Show children how to stick the photos to the cookie sheet. Can they name their friends? Can they match photos to the correct friend?

Older Influences. Invite an older class of children to come into the room and sing with infants. Babies will learn more from their slightly older counterparts than they ever will from you. Give it a try. You might find you develop more singers.

18+ Months

Friend Match. Give the children the Friendship Match Game (appendix page xxx) and encourage them to match the photos to their friends. Ask them to name their friends as they pair the pictures. When necessary, work with the infants to match the two photos. You might also encourage them to match the photos on the cards to their real friends. Or, make two enlarged copies of the photos. Glue one set of the photos inside a file folder. Glue the second set of photos on 3" x 5" index cards. Work with babies to match the two photos. You might also want to invite the children to match the photos on the cards to their real friends.

Classroom Greeter. Invite one of the infants to help you greet the other children as they arrive. If she is verbal have her say, "Hello." If your greeter is nonverbal, she can pat her classmates or hug them as they arrive.

Which Hand? Play a hand guessing game with babies. Place a button or a small toy in one of your hands. Place both hands behind your back and switch the toy back and forth. Hold both hands out in front of you and ask the babies to guess which hand is holding the toy. Older children may be able to take turns while playing the game with you.

Blowing Kisses. Teach the children how to blow a kiss. Teach the children to pretend to catch a kiss that is thrown to them.

Follow the Leader. Invite babies to play "Follow the Leader." For the first round of the game, you be the leader and let children mimic your actions. After they get the hang of it, let an older child take the lead.

Partner Clapping. Teach babies to clap hands with a partner. You will need to be the partner for most children. Teach those who are ready how to give a "high five."

Kiddie Cooks. Invite older infants to help prepare their meals. They can help wash fruit, take bread out of the wrapper, stir cool items, and put food on a plate.

Sharing Made Easier. When infants bring a toy from home, label it by writing their name on a piece of masking tape and sticking the tape to the item. To children possession is literally nine-tenths of the law. When their name is on their belonging they are less worried about who is holding the item because they feel that their name protects their rights.

Experiences and Activities to Develop Humor

Birth–18+ Months

Humor Words to Know. Teach children vocabulary words related to humor. Use the words in the chart below when appropriate and as often as you can.

Crazy	Ha-ha	Laugh	Tickle
Fun	Humor	Nutty	Wacky
Funny	Jolly	Silly	
Giggle		Smile	

Books on Humor. Read books that promote humor. Here are a few favorites:

Barnyard Dance! by Sandra Boynton
But Not the Hippopotamus by Sandra Boynton
Five Little Monkeys Jumping on the Bed by Eileen Christelow
Mr. Brown Can Moo, Can You? by Dr. Seuss
Sheep in a Jeep by Nancy E. Shaw
Tickle, Tickle by Helen Oxenbury
Where Is Baby's Belly Button? by Karen Katz

Crazy Clothes. Dress up in silly attire. Wear something unusual like a big floppy hat, a feather boa, or a pair of big sunglasses. This is a great diversion during diaper changing time. Describe what is silly about your attire.

Mirror Hat. Make a Mirror Hat (appendix page 231). Wear it when you change diapers. Ask infants if they can see themselves in the mirror. Encourage older infants to make a funny face.

Wacky Voices. Use funny voices with children from time to time. All age groups will respond to the novelty of your new voice. The voices of cartoon characters might serve as an inspiration for your funny voice. The more spontaneous you are, the more humorous your funny voice will be to infants.

Stuffed Laughers. Have on hand a variety of stuffed animals and toy characters that laugh. Laughing is contagious. A laughing stuffed friend will help make everyone gleeful.

Feather Duster Tickle. Use a clean feather duster to gently tickle infants. They will really enjoy it! Talk with them about the feel of the feathers. Say, *I'm going to get you. I'm tickling you. Gotcha!*

Red Nose. Place a red dot sticker on your nose. Who notices? Who thinks it's funny?

Birth–6 Months

Dance With Me, Baby. Dance with the baby. Play some bold music, hold her close, and dance with drama.

Socks on Hands. When an infant learns to watch her hand, add some novelty by putting a pair of colorful socks on her hands.

One, Two, Three. Count to three dramatically as you lift the baby from her crib or the floor. Lift on three. Place your hands on the baby on one, tighten them on two, and lift on three. Baby will learn to joyfully anticipate hearing "three."

Bellybutton Kisses. Kiss babies on their tummy. This is sure to get a laugh from babies between four and six months.

Bumblebee Buzz. Move one of your fingers around as if it were a bee trying to decide where to land. Make a buzzing sound to accompany your finger movements. Eventually land on baby's neck or tummy and lightly tickle.

Hummm? Wear insect antennae (available at party stores and seasonally at wholesale department stores) while you are tending to infants. They will love the novelty and the wackiness.

Canned Laughter. Record children laughing. Play the recording for babies. Does it make them smile?

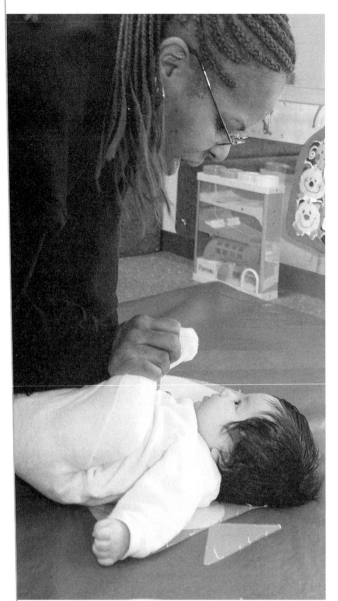

Toes to Nose. Lay an infant on her back. Lift her legs. Tap her toes together and then tap her toes on her nose. Recite "Toes to Nose" as you play. Add to your play with "Toes to Ears" (appendix page 214). Tap the baby's toes to her toes and then to her ears. Smile and laugh with her.

Toes to Nose

Toes to toes, that's how it goes.
Toes to nose, those silly toes!

Toes to toes, that's how it goes.
Toes to ears, those ears are dears!

Bella, Bella. Say the following rhyme with infants. They will learn to anticipate the "bruta, bruta, bruta."

Bella, Bella

Bella, bella, bella (say slowly while gently
    stroking baby's cheek)
    (hesitate)
Bruta, bruta, bruta (say rapidly while
    gently tapping baby's cheek)

Blanket Talk. Place a small lightweight blanket over the baby's head and your head. Talk to the baby under the blanket.

Jack-in-the-Box. Four- to six-month-olds are becoming comfortable in their surroundings and less likely to startle. Play a Jack-in-the-Box for the baby. Hold it about two feet away from her so she can see it well but not feel startled when it pops out of the box. Talk with her while you are waiting for Jack to appear. Let her know that something is going to happen by using your voice to build anticipation.

6–12 Months

A View From Up High. Take the infant for a ride on your shoulders. Talk with her about the new view.

'Round the House. Say the following "'Round the House" rhyme. Babies will learn to anticipate the under-the-arm tickle. For younger babies you may want to place the tickle on their neck instead of under their arm.

'Round the House
'Round the house, 'round the house (move your index finger around in a circle
   on baby's palm)
Goes the little mousie.
Up the stairs, up the stairs, (walk index finger and middle finger up baby's arm)
In the little housie. (gently tickle baby under her arm or on her neck)

Tummy Bounces. Lie on the floor and place the baby on your tummy. Hold her securely and bounce gently.

Flying High. Lie on your back and place the baby on your shins so she can see over your knees. Hold her hands and gently move your feet up and down. Say, *Look at you flying way up high.*

Finger Pal Puppets. Make Finger Pal Puppets (appendix page 228). Add funny little extras to the puppets, such as red yarn hair, wiggle eyes, a red pompom nose and so on. Use the puppets to talk to play and talk babies. **Safety Note:** Only caregivers should use Finger Pal Puppets. Be sure that babies do not put Finger Pal Puppets in their mouths.

Finger Creep. Creep fingers up the infant's leg to her chin and tickle. Watch for many smiles and laughs.

Baby Lifts. Lift baby up over your head. Move slowly with the first lift to ensure that baby is comfortable with this activity. Most babies love it and it is guaranteed to get a giggle.

Toe Tickles. Lay the baby on her back on the floor and remove her shoes. Gently touch her toes to her nose. Giggle. Touch baby's toes to her ears, and then giggle. Continue touching baby's body parts with her toes. Baby will laugh with you at each move.

Where's Your Bellybutton? Ask the baby to show you her bellybutton. Once she is able to find hers, don't be surprised if she "asks" to see (search for) yours.

Pat-a-Cake Humor. Play Pat-a-Cake with infants. Let your hands miss meeting each other on occasion. Act totally surprised at the miss. Try again. Miss again. Babies will find this very funny.

Pat-a-Cake
Pat-a-cake, pat-a-cake, baker's man. (clap hands together)
Bake me a cake as fast as you can.
Roll it (roll hands over each other)
And pat it (pat hands together)
And mark it with a "B." (draw a B in the air or on baby's tummy)
And put it in the oven for Baby and me. (tickle baby's tummy)

Whoops! Hold the baby's hand and touch each finger as you say "Johnny." Slide your finger between her forefinger and thumb and back again as you say "Whoops, Johnny." Touch the baby's fingers again on the remaining "Johnnys."

> **Whoops, Johnny**
> Johnny, Johnny
> Johnny, Johnny,
> Whoops, Johnny
> Whoops, Johnny
> Johnny, Johnny,
> Johnny.

Peek-a-Boo. Play Peek-a-Boo with infants. This classic game is a winner and a laugh producer every time.

Peek-a-Boo Surprises. Make a Surprise Board (appendix page 234). Place the board in front of the baby and play the game as you normally would. She will find it funny.

Peek-a-Boo Switcheroo. Cover the baby's face instead of yours to switch roles in the familiar Peek-a-Boo game.

Giddy-Up Horsie. Give babies a horsie ride. Sit in a chair, cross your legs, and let the baby sit on your foot. Hold her hand securely and bounce your leg up and down. Say, *Giddy-u,p horsie* and *Whoa, horsie* when appropriate. Say the "Ride a Little Horsie" rhyme below as you provide the baby with a horsie ride.

> **Ride a Little Horsie**
> Ride a little horsie,
> Go to town.
> Be very careful,
> So you don't fall down.

Crawling Mitts. Sew colorful pompoms on old socks or mittens. Add some jingle bells. Place them on baby's hands as they crawl. Help them see the humor by laughing and talking about how different it is to crawl with mitts on your hands. **Safety Note:** Make sure that you supervise this activity closely to make sure that the sewn-on items don't come loose.

Jack Surprises. Put a pair of miniature sunglasses or a doll's hat on your Jack-in-the-Box. Who laughs when Jack pops up?

6–18+ Months

Crawl With Me. Get on the floor and crawl with babies. They will get a kick out of your participation.

This Little Piggy. Take off a baby's shoe and touch her toes as you say "This Little Piggy."

This Little Piggy
This little piggy went to market, (wiggle big toe)
This little piggy stayed home, (wiggle second toe)
This little piggy had roast beef, (wiggle middle toe)
This little piggy had none, (wiggle fourth toe)
And this little piggy cried
"Wee-wee-wee!" all the way home. (wiggle little toe)

Head Pusher. Place a small, inflatable ball (8" diameter) on the floor. Show infants how to push the ball with her head as she crawls. Laugh with them as they move the ball across the floor.

THE COMPLETE RESOURCE BOOK FOR INFANTS

12–18+ Months

What's That Doing There? Move furniture into places it doesn't belong. Make a big deal about how the furniture got out of place. Make up a funny story about how the items got moved.

Hey! What's Happening? Change routines. Be spontaneous. Try eating dessert first. Take lunch outdoors. Remember routines offer children security. Make a big deal of changing the routine. Introduce the change like an exciting event. Talk about how things will change and point out the humor in being outside the norm.

Silly Me. Let children see you laugh at yourself. We all do silly things like getting our words mixed up or putting our shoes on the wrong feet, so we might as well laugh.

That's Funny! Sing silly songs and have a good laugh. Following are a few to enjoy. What babies like best are the "Peeee-eew!" "honk, honk," and so on!

> **Dirty Old Bill** (Tune: Turkey in the Straw)
> I know a man named Dirty Old Bill.
> He lives on top of a garbage hill.
> Oh, he never took a bath and he never will.
> Peeee-eew! Dirty Old Bill!

> **Little Hunk of Tin** (Tune: I'm a Little Acorn Brown)
> I'm a little hunk of tin.
> Nobody knows what shape I'm in.
> Got four wheels and a tank of gas.
> I can go but not too fast.

> Chorus:
> Honk, honk (pull ear)
> Rattle, rattle (shake head side to side)
> Crash, crash   (push chin)
> Beep, beep (push nose)
> (Repeat chorus twice.)

Little Ant's Hill (Tune: Dixie)

Oh, I stuck my foot	Oh, I didn't take it off,
On a little ant's hill,	And the little ant said,
And the little ant said,	"If you don't take it off
"You better be still,	You'll wish you had.
Take it off! Take it off!	Take it off! Take it off!"
Take it off! Remove it!"	Ouch! I removed it!

Tell a Tale of Humor. Read humorous books. Read them with enthusiasm. Here are some favorites for older infants.

Mr. Brown Can Moo, Can You? by Dr. Suess
The Monster at the End of This Book by Jon Stone
Wee Three Pigs by Heidi Petach
Tickle, Tickle by Helen Oxenbury
Where's Baby's Belly Button? by Karen Katz

Slowly, Slowly. Say the rhyme below with infants. This is also a great activity to reinforce opposites.

Slowly, Slowly
Slowly, slowly, very slowly (walk finger up arm slowly)
Creeps the garden snail.
Slowly, slowly, very slowly
Up the wooden rail.

Quickly, quickly, very quickly (run fingers up arm)
Runs the little mouse.
Quickly, quickly, very quickly
'Round about the house.

Got Your Nose. Play a game of pretending to snatch a baby's nose, toe, ear, and other parts of her body.

Jack in the Box. Obtain a large box large enough for you to hide inside. Sing "Pop Goes the Weasel" and pop out of the box when you get to the line, "Pop! Goes the weasel." After a while the children will want to be the "Jack" in the box. Allow them to play with in the box. Help older children be a "Jack" in the box.

Pop! Goes the Weasel

All around the mulberry bush,
The monkey chased the weasel.
The weasel thought it was all in
fun,
Pop! Goes the weasel.

A penny for a spool of thread,
A penny for a needle,
That's the way the money goes—
Pop! Goes the weasel.

All around the mulberry bush,
The monkey chased the weasel.
The weasel thought it was all in
fun,
Pop! Goes the weasel.

Toe Wiggle. Have everyone take of their shoes and wiggle their toes. Put on some music and wiggle to the music. Paint a face on your big toe and let it talk to the children.

Tightrope Walking. Make a line on the floor with masking tape. Encourage babies to walk the line. For variety, have children walk a crooked line or walk the line with a beanbag on their head.

Funny Hats. Make Funny Hats (appendix page 229). Take the hats out occasionally and let the children wear them. They will laugh at each other. Be sure to have a mirror available so infants can see their Funny Hats.

Shoes on My Hands? Give babies soft shoes to wear on their hands as they crawl around the floor.

Absurd Antics. Do silly things designed to make babies laugh, such as pick up one of the children's shoes and pretend you are trying to put it on your foot or pick up an item of doll's clothing and pretend you are going to put the item on. Children will get a big kick out of your antics.

Silly Hide and Seek. Encourage babies to hide from you. When you look for them, look in silly places like inside drawers and in the sink (down the drain) and other places that are way too small.

Kiss My Foot. Sit on the floor with a baby and tell her you are going to kiss her feet. Kiss both feet. When she laughs say, *Do you want to kiss my foot?* Pretend that you are going to take your shoe off and let her kiss your foot. She will find your offer funny.

Piggy Play. Play "This Little Piggy" with a baby's feet. After a few rounds, ask the baby if she would like to count your "piggies." You can also play this game with fingers. Either way, she will be amused by touching your piggy toes or piggy fingers.

Which Hand? Place a small object in one of your hands while you hide them behind your back. Hold your hands out in front of you and ask babies to guess which hand holds the surprise.

18+ Months

Toe Pick Up. Place several one-inch pompoms (available in craft stores) on the floor. Have the children take off their shoes. Challenge them to pick up the pompoms with their toes. **Safety Note:** Supervise closely. Be sure that the children do not put the pompoms in their mouths.

Purposeful Mistakes. Play games with children substituting words that are nonsensical. For example, say, *I'm going to get your ear* while you gently grab the baby's toe. Does she notice your "mistake?"

Silly Thing. Once children understand the proper way things work, do them a silly way. For example, put a shoe on your hand, turn a picture upside down, tie a bow on a baby's glass of juice, or turn a table upside down. Do the children understand the humor?

Silly Magic. Make a Magic Wand (appendix page 231). Tell infants that when you point the wand at them, they must do something silly.

Don't Laugh. Play "Don't Laugh" with infants. Do funny things such as act like you are getting ready to tickle the children and all the while keep saying *Don't you laugh!* Not laughing will be next to impossible. Solicit the participation of another adult to take on the role of the children. Your accomplice will help get the laughter going.

Stop! Play a swinging game on the playground. Swing the baby. Tell her you are going to play a "Stop and Go" game. When she is away from your hands and at the height of her swing say, *Stop.* Of course she can't. When she reaches the height of her swing a second time say, *Hey, Stop right there!* As she descends back toward you say, in a teasing voice, *I thought I told you to stop.* Does she laugh? Say, *Let's try it again.* Continue as long as babies think it is funny.

Chapter 3

Physical Development—
Moving and Exploring

Overview

Infants are born with very little muscle control because they have been in a cramped space for nine months. Most movements that infants make are more a function of automatic reflex than actual control. However, once baby arrives, wiring for muscle control is a high priority.

Motor development is wired during the first two years of life (Ramey & Ramey, 1999). This occurs through experience and is strengthened by repeated experience. Between birth and two, children need experiences that support the wiring of both the small muscles (fingers, toes, face, and eyes) and the large muscles (arms, legs, abdomen, back, and neck) of their bodies. They need plenty of space, plenty of things to touch and explore, and plenty of freedom to move. There is a direct correlation between freedom to move and the agility and dexterity that child will possess as an adult.

During the first two years, infants will vary greatly in how much muscle control they demonstrate. Some babies will hold their head up within a couple of weeks. Others will not hold their head up for a month or more. Some babies will be able to hold their head steady within a couple of months, others will need another month or two. One of the obvious differences in how infants develop muscle control can be seen around the fifth or sixth month. Some babies will be crawling while others are still trying to learn to sit. These differences are normal and should not be used to evaluate children's capabilities. By age two, most motor differences in motor development have disappeared.

Fine Motor

Fine motor activities include pinching, squeezing, tearing, rolling, grasping, tossing, catching, pounding, smiling, tracking, opening and closing fingers, creeping fingers, coordinating hand and eyes, and more. Early experiences need to include opportunities to practice all of these activities.

Gross Motor

Gross motor activities include walking, running, jumping, twisting, turning, hopping, hugging, pushing, pulling, dancing, and much more. Early experiences need to include opportunities to practice all of these activities. Because gross motor activities, unlike fine motor activities, are basically whole body activities, children need open space to move and materials and equipment that promote gross motor activities, such as tunnels, rocking toys, riding toys, and climbing apparatus.

Experiences and Activities to Develop Fine Motor Skills

Birth–18+ Months

Fine Motor Words to Know. Teach infants vocabulary words related to small muscles and fine motor skills. Use the words in the chart below when appropriate.

Button	Hold	Squeeze	Twist
Carry	Open	Throw	Unwrap
Catch	Pick up	Thumb	Wiggle
Close	Pinch	Tie	Wrap
Fingers	Pull	Toes	Wrist
Grasp	Push	Track	Zip
Hands	Smile	Turn	

Books About Fine Motor Development. Read books that promote fine motor activities and concepts. Here are some favorites:

Clap Your Hands by Lorinda Bryan Cauley
Hand, Hand, Finger, Thumb by Al Perkin
Here Are My Hands by Bill Martin, Jr. and John Archambault
Piggies by Audrey Wood
Ten Little Fingers by Annie Kubler

Birth–6 Months

Finger Grasp. Encourage babies to practice grasping. Place your finger in a baby's palm. He will grasp your finger by automatic reflex. Encourage him to continue holding your finger. Say the "Grasping Rhyme," if you like.

Grasping Rhyme
I place my finger in your left palm.
You grab it and hold on tight.
Your left hand is growing stronger.
Now let's try it with your right.

Get My Finger. While feeding a baby, hold a finger in front of him and encourage him to grab it.

Sponge Squeeze. Give infants soft sponges to hold and squeeze. The smaller the sponge the better, but be sure that the sponges are too large to swallow. **Safety Note:** Supervise closely to ensure that infants don't bite off pieces of sponges.

Grasping Games. Play grasping games with infants. Offer the baby a small plush toy or rattle to reach for and grasp. Change the locations of where you hold the toy. Start at a close distance and gradually move a little further away. Hold it to the baby's left and then his right.

"This Little Piggy" Fingers. Do "This Little Piggy" (appendix page 213) using baby's fingers instead of his toes.

Here Comes the Airplane. When feeding an infant, play "Here Comes the Airplane." Hold a bite of food on his spoon about 12" from his face and make it soar slowly like a plane. Gradually move toward his face and when you get to his mouth say, *In the hangar it goes.* This is a great visual tracking activity.

Sensory Glove. Give infants a Sensory Glove (appendix page 233). Encourage them to squeeze the fingers. **Safety Note:** Supervise closely to ensure that infants don't bite off pieces of the glove.

Follow This. Move a rattle slowly from left to right in front of a baby—about 14" from his face. Does he follow the rattle with his eyes? Repeat this activity often. When baby gets good at following (tracking) the rattle, try increasing the distance from his face.

Watch the Rattle. Place a baby on his stomach. Face him and dangle a rattle directly in front of his face. Slowly lift the rattle so that he has to raise his head to follow it. Encourage him to use his arms to push up. Celebrate his success.

Follow the Ball. Lay the baby on his tummy, or if he can sit up, put him in a sitting position. Roll a ball in front of him. Say, *Watch the ball.* Is he able to keep his eyes on the ball? Play the game several times. This activity will help him with his visual tracking.

Hand Pals. Give baby Canister Shakers (appendix page 226). These little shakers are a perfect size—easy to grasp and big enough not to be swallowed. Give infants a Canister Shaker for each hand. It will help develop their grasp. For a variation, hand the baby Canister Bells (appendix page 226).

Finger Watching. Put the baby in a position where he can see you well. Sit in front of him and sing songs with finger movements, such as "Where Is Thumbkin?" and "Five Little Fingers." Additional fingerplays are in the appendix on pages 199–203.

> **Where Is Thumbkin?** (Traditional)
> Where is Thumbkin? (hands behind back)
> Where is Thumbkin?
> Here I am. Here I am. (bring out right thumb, then left)
> How are you today, sir? (bend right thumb)
> Very well, I thank you. (bend left thumb)
> Run away. Run away. (put right thumb behind back, then left thumb
>   behind back)
>
> Other verses:
> Where is Pointer?
> Where is Middle One?
> Where is Ring Finger?
> Where is Pinky?
> Where are all of them?

Five Little Fingers

One little finger standing on its own. (hold up index finger)

Two little fingers, now they're not alone. (hold up middle finger)

Three little fingers happy as can be. (hold up ring finger)

Four little fingers go walking down the street. (hold up all fingers)

Five little fingers. This one is a thumb. (hold up four fingers and thumb)

Wave bye-bye 'cause now we are done. (wave bye-bye)

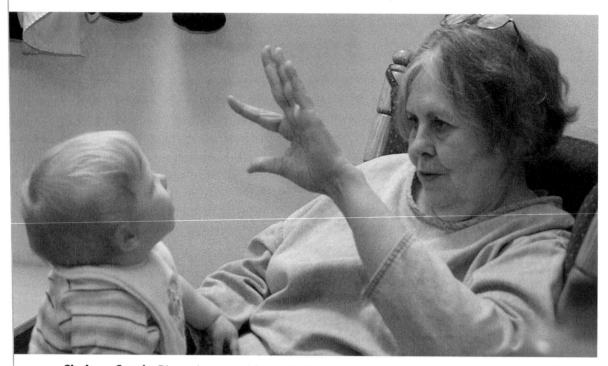

Shake a Snack. Place dry cereal in a plastic bottle and encourage infants to shake their snack out of the bottle and onto their tray.

Beautiful Bubbles. Blow bubbles for infants and encourage them to watch the bubbles float away. This will help strengthen visual tracking. Sing to the infants as you watch the bubbles.

Bubble Song by Pam Schiller (Tune: K-K-K-Katie)

B-B-B-Bubbles, beautiful bubbles,

Will you float upon the air or will you soar?

B-B-B-Bubbles, beautiful bubbles,

Oh, it's b-b-b-bubbles we adore.

B-B-B-Bubbles, beautiful bubbles,

Blow just a few and you'll want more.

B-B-B-Bubbles, beautiful bubbles,

Oh, it's b-b-b-bubbles we adore.

6–12 Months

Scarf Pull. Make a Scarf Pull (appendix page 233) and give it to infants to explore.

Feely Box Fun. Make a Feely Box (appendix page 228). Encourage infants to feel the items inside the box.

Paper Crunch. Give infants paper to crunch and tear. Supervise closely so that bits of paper don't end up in their mouths.

Slot Drop Can. Make a Slot Drop Can (appendix page 233) and invite infants to explore dropping the chips or buttons in the can. Supervise closely to ensure that children do not put the chips or buttons in their mouths.

Spoon on a String. Cut a 24" piece of yarn. Tie one end of the yarn around the baby's spoon and the other end of the yarn to the baby's feeding table. When baby tosses his spoon, show him how to retrieve it.

Goop Bags. Mix a batch of Goop (appendix page 222). Place a ball of Goop in a resealable plastic bag and glue the bag shut. Give the Goop Bag to the infants and encourage them to squeeze the bag, flatten the bag, twist the bag, and so on. **Safety Note:** Supervise closely to ensure that infants don't bite off pieces of the bag.

Squish, Squash. Place sliced bananas on children's feeding trays. Can they pick up the slippery slices?

Ball Bounce. Bounce a ball across the floor in front of the baby. Does he follow the ball?

Gelatin Jigglers. Give babies Gelatin Jigglers (appendix page 219). Are they able to pick up the jigglers? Talk with them about the feel of the gelatin. Recite the following "Gelatin Jiggler Rhyme" while the children eat their Jigglers. **Note:** Provide sweet treats to children in moderation. Large amounts of sugar are not conducive to keeping the brain alert, and the only thing we get from sugar is calories.

> **Gelatin Jiggler Rhyme** by Pam Schiller
> Gelatin Jigglers in my tummy.
> Gelatin Jigglers yummy, yummy, yummy.
> Gelatin Jigglers wiggle, jiggle, wiggle.
> Galatin Jigglers make me giggle.

Trail Mix. Let "cooking helpers" assist you in making Trail Mix (appendix page 219). Serve the Trail Mix on feeding trays. How easily can babies pick up the items in the mix? It is all just the right size for little fingers.

Spider Fingers. Sing "Itsy Bitsy Spider" (appendix page 190). Show children how to wiggle their fingers like spiders as you sing. For a variation, try making spider shadow puppets by wiggling your fingers like a spider between the wall and a light source. Older children may be able to make shadow spider puppets with you.

Button, Zip, and Snap. Provide articles of clothing that fasten with snaps, zippers, and buttons. Challenge infants to work with the fasteners.

12–18+ Months

Fill, Dump, and Eat. At snack time, give infants plastic cups and dry cereal to pick up and put into their cups.

Wiggles. Do "I Wiggle" with babies. Before you say the rhyme, identify, or have infants identify, each body part mentioned in the rhyme. Show children how to wiggle.

> ### I Wiggle
> I wiggle, wiggle, wiggle my fingers. (wiggle fingers)
> I wiggle, wiggle, wiggle my toes. (wiggle toes)
> I wiggle, wiggle, wiggle my shoulders. (wiggle shoulders)
> I wiggle, wiggle, wiggle my nose. (wiggle nose)
> Now no more wiggles are left in me, (shake head)
> I am sitting as still as still can be. (sit still)

Gooey, Gooey, Goop. Mix a batch of Goop (appendix page 222). Show the children how to punch, pound, and twist it. Supervise play closely so babies don't put the Goop in their mouths. Talk with the babies while they play. Describe the texture of the Goop. Ask them how they think the Goop feels.

What's Inside? Wrap some small toys in wrapping paper or in boxes and let the children unwrap them. Talk about what's inside. Help older infants guess what might be inside.

Slip It In. Make a slot that is 10" long and 1" wide in the top of a box similar to a copy paper box. Give the children six-inch paper or plastic plates to drop into the box.

Tape Removal. Place several strips of masking tape on a tabletop, tray, or on the floor. Show infants how to pull up the strips. **Safety Note:** Supervise closely to ensure that pieces of tape don't end up in a baby's mouth. Be sure to discard all tape when this activity is over.

Open, Shut Them. Sing "Open, Shut Them" with the children. Suit actions to the words of the song. Talk about all the wonderful things the children can do by opening and shutting their hands, such as carrying a small item or waving "goodbye."

Open, Shut Them

Open, shut them.
Open, shut them.
Give a little clap.

Open, shut them.
Open, shut them.
Put them in your lap.

Walk them, walk them, (walk fingers up chest to chin)
Walk them, walk them.
Way up to your chin.

Walk them, walk them, (walk fingers around face, but not into mouth)
Walk them, walk them,
But don't let them walk in.

Water Play. Provide a tub of water, sponges, basters, bars of soap (no-tear soap), washcloths, and cups for children to play with. Talk with them about what each item is and how it works. Limit participants to two at a time and supervise closely.

Washing Rocks. Provide a tub of water, soap, sponges, and rocks or shells. Talk with them as they work. *Look, the rocks are changing colors when they get wet! They are darker when they are wet. I like this rock that is round and smooth. Which rock do you like the best?* **Safety Note:** Be sure the rocks or shells are large enough so they cannot be swallowed and that they have no sharp edges). Invite young archeologists to wash the rocks and/or shells.

Tongs Pick Up. Give infants tongs and some small items to pick up. Some children will be proficient at using tongs. Encourage them to place the items they pick up in a box or bucket.

Pass the Beanbag. Have the children sit in a circle. Play some music and have the children pass a beanbag around and around the circle. It is easy for us, but it takes a great deal of dexterity for the children to pass a beanbag to one another.

Fingerplays. Here are some simple fingerplays you can teach infants. See pages 199–203 in the appendix for more fingerplays.

Fabulous Fingers by Pam Schiller
My fingers are so fabulous, (hold hands up)
Just look what they can do.
They can wiggle, they can dance, (wiggle fingers)
And take a bow or two. (fold fingers at knuckle)
They can wave, they can point, (wave)
And even blow a kiss. (blow on hand)
But what they like most— (hold a friend's hand)
Is to hold a hand like this.

Five Little Fingers
One little finger standing on its own. (hold up index finger)
Two little fingers, now they're not alone. (hold up middle finger)
Three little fingers happy as can be. (hold up ring finger)
Four little fingers go walking down the street. (hold up all fingers)
Five little fingers. This one is a thumb. (hold up four fingers and thumb)
Wave bye-bye 'cause now we are done. (wave bye-bye)

Stringing Tubes. Cover empty toilet paper tubes with contact paper. Cut the tubes into 2"-3" pieces. Show infants how to string the tubes onto a thick piece of yarn. Wrap one end of the yarn with masking tape to create a "needle." Tie the other end of the yarn around one of the tubes to create a stopper.

Twinkle, Twinkle. Sing "Twinkle, Twinkle, Little Star" (appendix page 197). Model holding your hands above your head and opening and closing your fingers. In no time at all, you will have a sky full of little twinkling stars.

Pompom Pick Up. Place 2" pompoms (available in craft stores) on a carpet square. Give babies a bucket and encourage them to pick up the pompoms and place them in the bucket or pail. Supervise closely to ensure that babies don't put items in their mouths.

Coaster Bank. Cut a 4" x ½" slot in the top of a plastic lid of a 5-pound coffee can. Give the children plastic coasters to drop through the slot.

Soap It Up. Provide a tub of water and different size bars of soap. Invite the babies to enjoy the feel of the soap in their hands as they explore the bars of soap.

Drop the Beanbag. Provide a bucket and a beanbag. Show the infants how to stand over the bucket, hold the beanbag at waist height, and drop it into the bucket. When the children get good at hitting the bucket when holding the beanbag at that height, encourage them to try raising the beanbag to their chests and dropping it.

Dress-Up Clothes. Provide dress-up clothes for children to explore. Include items that snap, button, and zip. Be sure to provide a mirror.

Finger Puppets. Invite the infants to play with Finger Pal Puppets (appendix page 228). Encourage them to wear two of three of the puppets and to move them when they talk.

Shakers. Fill saltshakers with colored sand (appendix page 226). Invite the infants to shake the sand onto a piece of butcher paper. They love watching the sand fall onto the paper. Or, provide construction paper with glue brushed over it for the children to use as a landing spot for the colored sand. Then, they can keep the sand as their own work of art.

Jars and Lids. Give babies plastic jars and lids to play with. They love to screw and unscrew the lids. Take all the lids off and see if the children can match lids to their jars.

Ball Holders. Give infants tennis balls and a large muffin tin. Challenge them to place one ball in each cup.

Clap Your Hands. With the children, say rhymes that include movements that require the use of their small muscles. Here are a few examples. There are other examples in the appendix (see pages 204–215).

> **Clap Your Hands** (suit actions to words)
> Clap your hands 1-2-3.
> Clap your hands just like me.
> Wiggle your fingers 1-2-3.
> Wiggle your fingers just like me.

> **Two Little Houses**
> Two little houses,
> Closed up tight. (close fists)
> Let's open the windows,
> And let in some light. (open fists)
> And let in the light.

Shake Your Pudding. Invite babies to help you make Individual Pudding (appendix page 219). Recite "Shake Your Pudding" while everyone shakes.

> **Shake Your Pudding** by Pam Schiller
>
> Shake, shake, shake your pudding.
> Shake it here, shake it there.
> Shake it everywhere.
>
> Shake, shake, shake your pudding.
> Shake it high, shake it low.
> Shake it head to toe.
>
> Shake, shake, shake your pudding.
> Shake it front. Shake it back.
> Shake it like a sack.
>
> Shake, shake, shake your pudding.
> Shake it here, shake it there.
> Shake it everywhere!

Turn the Page. Encourage children to help you turn the pages of a book.

Squirt Bottle Fun. Fill a spray bottle with water and let children who are 16 months and older use it outdoors. You can plan on getting wet—it won't take long for you to become their favorite target!

18+ Months

Frog Gobblers. Give the children Frog Gobblers (appendix page 229). Encourage them to use the Frog Gobblers to pick up pompoms and drop them into a bowl. Most babies will feel more comfortable using two hands to operate the Gobbler.

Big Bubbles. Provide a shallow tub of Bubble Soap (appendix page 220). Give the children large wands and other bubble-making instruments, such as plastic six-pack holders, commercial blowers, and strainers.

Bubbles in My Hand. Provide a tub of soapy water. Show children how to blow bubbles using your fist as a bubble shaper. Make a loose fist and rub soapy water around your index finger and thumb. Blow through the hole created by your index finger and thumb. Large bubbles can be made this way. Challenge children to blow bubbles through their fists. Several will be good at bubble blowing, and others will enjoy trying.

Twisties. Give infants fat pipe cleaners to twist into whatever shapes they choose.

Eyedropper Transfer. Provide large eyedroppers and a small tub of water. Challenge infants to use the eyedroppers to move the water from the tub to a cup. Demonstrate pinching the bulb of the eyedropper to pick up the water. This activity offers a great opportunity for using spatial vocabulary. Use appropriate vocabulary with children as they work, for example, *up, down, in, out*, and other related words.

Ball Catch. Toss soft balls and challenge children to catch them. Talk with the children about keeping their eyes on the ball.

Experiences and Activities to Develop Gross Motor Skills

Birth–18+ Months

Gross Motor Words to Know. Teach children vocabulary words related to large muscles and gross motor skills. Use the words in the chart below when appropriate and as often as you can.

Arms	Foot	Pedal	Sway
Bend	Head	Pull	Throw
Catch	Hop	Push	Toes
Chase	Jump	Roll	Toss
Crawl	Kick	Run	Walk
Dance	Knee	Shoulder	
Exercise	Leg	Sit	
Feet	Move	Stand	

Read About Gross Motor Development. "Young explorers" will enjoy books that promote gross motor activities and concepts. Here are a few suggestions:

Baby Dance by Ann Taylor
The Baby Dances by Kathy Henderson
Clap Hands by Helen Oxenbury
From Head to Toe by Eric Carle
Toddlerobics by Zita Newcome

Freedom to Roam. Make sure that every baby has freedom to roam every day.

Stand Up, Sit Down. Play "Stand Up, Sit Down." With young infants and "not yet walkers" hold them in your lap facing you. Say, "Stand up" and pull upward to help the baby stand. Say, "Sit down" and release your pull so that it cues the baby to sit. With older children, start by alternating stand up and sit down commands, but then repeat a command to add a little humor and fun to the game. **Safety Note:** Provide appropriate support to baby at all times.

Cross-Lateral Movements. Do cross-lateral movements daily—several times a day if possible. Cross-lateral movements require the individual to reach across the midline (defined as an invisible line between the nose and the navel) with either arms or legs. Cross-lateral movement helps develop the cells between the hemispheres of the brain. Good cell integration (development) results in better left brain-right brain communication. Here are some suggestions for ways to incorporate cross-lateral movements into a baby's routine.

- Take a minute during a diaper change to move baby's arms and legs across his body.
- Encourage crawling during playtime.
- During lunchtime, arrange cups for older children so that reaching for the cup requires reaching across their midlines.

Birth–6 Months

Hi, Baby. Lie on the floor and place the baby on your chest. When he lifts his head to look at you, talk to him. Tell him you are happy to be taking care of him and will always try to be sure he is comfortable and happy.

Tactile Tug of Fun. Provide a variety of materials to use as a rope, such as scarves, thick yarn, cording, or small towels, in a game of Tug of Fun. Talk to baby about the feel of each type of "rope" as you play a tugging game. **Safety Note:** Make sure that "ropes" are put away after play.

Pillow Kick. Place a pillow at the baby's feet during playtime. He will enjoy kicking the soft surface. Remove the pillow when playtime is over.

Pat-a-Cake Feet. Play "Pat-a-Cake" (appendix page 210) using the baby's feet instead of his hands.

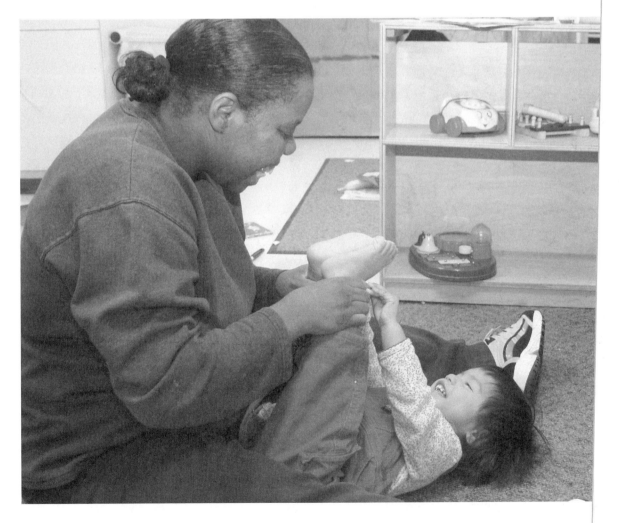

Baby Bicycle. Place the infant on his back and move his legs in a bicycle motion.

Tube Swings. Suspend empty toilet paper or paper towel tubes from a mobile. Show him how to swing the tubes by batting them with his hands. Supervise closely at all times.

Baby Pull-Up. Sit a baby in your lap facing you. Hold his hands and give him a slight tug. He will stand up. Do several pull-ups. Lay baby on his back and give his hands a slight tug. See if he will stand from this position. **Safety Note:** As with any activity, do not force the baby to move until he is developmentally ready for the movement.

Gaining Control. Infants spend the first few months of life working to gain control of their necks and heads. Lay the baby on his tummy. Place an interesting toy in front of him and encourage him to lift his head to look at the toy.

Sit Up Practice. Place a baby in your lap with his feet towards your stomach and his head at your knees. Hold his hands and gently pull him toward you. He will sit up. Do the exercise several times. It will strengthen baby's back and will also get him used to the sitting position. **Safety Note:** As with any activity, do not force a baby to move until he is developmentally ready for the movement.

Sitting. Between four and six months, infants are learning to sit. Practice helps. Place babies on a carpeted area of the room and surround them with pillows. Sit with them and talk to them so they will have something to focus on while they practice sitting.

Blanket Roll. During outdoor time, place a blanket on a grassy area. Lay the baby on the blanket on his tummy. Gently and carefully lift one side of the blanket to encourage baby to roll from his tummy to his back. Celebrate the roll with a big hug.

Exercise Time. Move baby's arms and legs to the rhyme below.

> **Exercise Time**
> Arms up, 1-2-3.
> Arms out, 1-2-3.
> Arms together, 1-2-3.
> Arms down, 1-2-3.
> Legs up, 1-2-3.
> Legs out, 1-2-3.
> Legs together, 1-2-3.
> Legs down, 1-2-3.

Photo Display. Make a Photo Box (appendix page 232). Place the baby on his tummy and sit the Photo Box beside him or in front of him, so he can lift his head to see the photographs. Turn the box occasionally for a new visual experience. You might also display older children's artwork inside the Photo Box.

Heads Up. Lay the infant on his stomach with a pillow under his chest. The pillow encourages him to lift his head.

6–12 Months

Crawling Buddies. Get on the floor and crawl beside an infant. Crawl a few steps and then beckon him to follow. Explore the room this way. Talk about things you see.

Bumpy Car Ride. Lie on your back. Let baby straddle your stomach while you bump up and down. Support baby as needed.

Horsie Ride. Lie on your back, raise your legs, and bend your knees. Position the baby on your shins. Hold his hands and support baby as you gently bounce him up and down.

Tunnel Fun. Construct a Box Tunnel (appendix page 225). Encourage babies to crawl through the box. Use only one box with beginning crawlers.

Bubble Fun. Blow bubbles (recipe on page 220) for babies. Younger children can reach for the bubbles and "walkers" can chase them. Sing the "Bubble Song" (appendix page 186) while you blow.

Diaper Derby. Make a start and finish line on the floor with masking tape. Place two crawlers on the start line and then move to the finish line and call infants to you. Who gets there first? Who isn't interested?

Walking With My Baby. Encourage the children who are on the verge of walking by holding their hands and walking them around the room. Work with another adult to let "beginning walkers" practice by walking between the two of you. Encourage "beginning walkers" to walk around a table or a chair. **Safety Note:** Stand beside "beginning walkers" to make sure they don't slip.

Field of Pillows. Toss several pillows on the floor to create an obstacle course for crawlers to crawl through. Some will crawl over the pillows.

Pounding Bench. Provide a pounding bench and let infants pound away.

Crawling, Crawling. Invite crawlers to crawl forward and then backward. Can anyone do it? Get down on the floor and crawl with them. Demonstrate the two directions. Reinforce the vocabulary words "forward" and "backward."

Leg Exercises. Lay the infant on the floor on his back. Exercise his legs as if he were riding a bicycle. Sing "This Is the Way We Kick Our Legs."

This Is the Way We Kick Our Legs (Tune: "Here We Go 'Round the
   Mulberry Bush)
This is the way we kick our legs,
Kick our legs, kick our legs.
This is the way we kick our legs,
To make them sure and strong.

Rock and Go. Crawl on the floor with crawlers. Try to get them to rock with you before they take off. Say the "Rock and Go Crawl Chant" for inspiration.

Rock and Go Crawl Chant

Rock, rock, rock,

Go, go, go.

Rock, rock, rock,

To and fro.

Go, go, go,

Just like so.

Rock, rock,

Go, go!

12–18+ Months

Here We Go. Say the following rhyme "Here We Go" and challenge infants to move as directed by the words.

Here We Go

Here we go—up, up, up. (stand up on toes)

Here we go—down, down, down. (crouch down)

Here we go—moving forward. (take a step forward)

Here we go—moving backward. (take a step backward)

Here we go 'round and 'round and 'round (spin)

Walk the Line. Make a line of masking tape on the floor. Encourage "walkers" to walk the line. Older infants may be able to walk the line with a bean bag on their head. Some infants will be able to jump up and down along the line.

Paper Bag Blocks. Make a set of Paper Bag Blocks (appendix page 232). Invite children to stack the blocks and then knock them down.

Bubble Chase. Blow bubbles and encourage the babies to chase them. Sing the "Bubble Song" or "Bubbles in the Air" to the tune of "K-K-K-Katie."

> **Bubble Song** by Pam Schiller (Tune: K-K-K-Katie)
> B-B-B-Bubbles, beautiful bubbles.
> We love you more and more and more and more and more.
> B-B-B-Bubbles, beautiful bubbles.
> You're the b-b-b-b-bubbles we adore.

> **Bubbles in the Air** by Pam Schiller (Tune: If You're Happy and You Know It)
> Bubbles in the air, in the air! (run, run, run)
> Bubbles in the air, in the air! (run, run, run)
> Bubbles in the air
> Bubbles everywhere
> Bubbles in the air, in the air! (run, run, run)

Through the Tunnels. Cut arches in both sides of large boxes and place them in an open space in the room. Even if children are walking, encourage them to crawl through the tunnels. Place several boxes together to make a longer tunnel. For added fun, create a tunnel with a couple of turns.

Mazes. Use tables and chairs to make a maze. Invite the infants to crawl through the maze.

Crawling Path. Cut 4" diameter circles out of colored contact paper and arrange them in a path. Invite the infants to crawl along the pathway. Encourage them to place their hands on the circles.

Big Steps. Place sheets of construction paper or strips of colored tape about 8" apart in a pathway on the floor. Encourage babies to step with one foot then the other on the pathway.

Giant Steps, Baby Steps. Make a start and finish line with masking tape. Show infants how to take baby steps, and then help them take baby steps from the start line to the finish line. Then show the children how to take giant steps. Have them take giant steps from the start line to the finish line. *Which step is more fun? Why? Why are the big steps called "giant" steps? Why are the small steps called "baby" steps?* Help infants answer the questions.

THE COMPLETE RESOURCE BOOK FOR INFANTS

Bouncing Ball. Show the children how a ball bounces. Tell them you want them to pretend to be bouncing balls. Say the following chant as they bounce in place.

> **Bouncing Ball**
> I'm bouncing, bouncing, bouncing everywhere.
> I bounce and bounce into the air.
> I'm bouncing, bouncing like a ball.
> I bounce and bounce until I fall. (children drop to the floor)

Pick Up and Dump. Give the infants plastic pails and shovels. Make some paper balls with waded up newspaper and place them on the floor. Encourage them to pick up the paper balls with their shovels and place them in the pails.

Beanbag Toss. Place a box in the middle of the floor and encourage the babies to toss beanbags into the box.

Sleigh Pull. Make a sleigh by attaching a rope (to pull with) to a shallow cardboard box. Help the children load their sleigh with stuffed animals or soft blocks and then encourage them to pull the sleigh around the room. Older children may enjoy having a "loading dock" and a "delivery area" to enhance their play.

Scarf Dancing. Give each child a scarf or a streamer (12" or shorter). Play some music and encourage the little dancers to dance. Use Streamer Rings (appendix page 234) for a variation.

Ball Kick. Suspend a beach ball from the ceiling to a distance of 12" to 15" from the floor. Show infants how to lie on their backs under the ball and kick it with their feet.

May I Have This Dance? Play some music or sing a song and let the children take turns standing on your feet and holding your hands while you dance. This is a great activity to encourage balance and coordination.

Bubble Stomp. Give the children small sheets of large bubble wrap. Show them how to stomp on the wrap to pop the bubbles. Older infants may be able to pop the bubbles with their fingers. Show them how. **Safety Note:** Taping the sheets of bubble wrap to the floor will make it less likely that the children will slip on them. Also, supervise closely so children do not put the bubble wrap in their mouths.

Log Rolls. Show the infants how to lie on the floor and roll like a log. As they get good at rolling, use masking tape to make two parallel lines on the floor about 4' apart and challenge them to roll between the lines.

Slipper Walkers. Collect old slippers from families. Invite the walkers to select a pair of slippers and put them on for a walk. Many infants will enjoy wearing the slippers on their hands and crawling around the room. Either way they are exercising their large muscles. **Safety Note:** Provide support to children who need it.

Classroom Soccer. Turn a laundry basket on its side and encourage young soccer players to kick a foam ball or an inflatable ball into the basket.

Teacher's Helpers. On a sunny day, take the classroom chairs outdoors and invite the babies to help you wash them. Provide soapy water and sponges. Ask families to bring a swimsuit for their child to wear.

Jumpers. Place two or three strips of masking tape on a carpeted area of the room and encourage "young jumpers" to jump over the pieces of tape. The following is a rhyme you can say to accompany their jumping.

> **Jumping Rhyme**
> Jump, jump, jump, my dear.
> Starting there and ending here.

Carwash. During outdoor play, provide a bucket of soapy water, sponges, and a few plastic riding toys. Encourage the infants to wash the "cars."

Partner Ball Play. Sit two children on the floor facing each other with their legs spread. Give them a ball and show them how to roll the ball back and forth to each other.

Under the Sheet. Have other adults help hold a sheet in an open position. Lift the sheet high so it catches the air and then while still holding the sheet let it float down. Encourage the children to run under the sheet while it is floating down.

Let's March. Play some marching music and teach babies to march. Start by just marching in place. When they improve at marching, you can march all around the room.

Five Little Monkeys. Encourage the children to jump while you recite "Five Little Monkeys". Talk about why the monkey fell off the bed. Tell the children that they should never jump on the bed.

Five Little Monkeys

Five little monkeys jumping on the bed.
One fell off and bumped her head.
Mama called the doctor, and the
   doctor said,
"No more monkeys jumping on the bed!"
(Repeat, subtracting a monkey each time.
Say the rhyme using fingers or act it out.)

Pop Goes the Weasel. Play "Pop! Goes the Weasel" (appendix page 193) with children. Soon some of the children will be able to yell, "Pop!" with you.

Indoor Golfing. Provide empty paper towel tubes, tennis balls (or similar size foam balls) and empty gallon ice cream cartons for a game of indoor golf. Cut the ice cream container in half vertically. Place the ice cream container in a pathway about five feet apart. Show infants how to use the empty paper towel tubes as clubs to hit the tennis balls into the ice cream cartons.

Stretching Fun. Do some stretching exercises with infants. Stretch to the chants below.

Stretching Fun

I stretch and stretch and find it fun (stretch)
To try to reach up to the sun. (reach hands up)
I bend and bend to touch the ground, (touch the ground)
Then I twist and twist around. (twist side to side)

Stretching Chant (suit actions to words)
Stretch to the windows,
Stretch to the door,
Stretch up to the ceiling,
And bend to the floor.

Spider Walk. Teach children how to walk like spiders. Have them bend at the waist and walk on all fours. Play some "spider-walking music" and encourage children to "spider walk."

Drop the Bead in the Box. Provide large beads and a box. Challenge children to drop the beads in the box.

Animal Antics. Demonstrate animal behaviors and encourage the children to copy you. Stretch like a cat. Shake like a dog. Waddle like a duck. Roar like a lion. Jump like a monkey. Hop like a frog. Flap your wings like a bird.

Frog Jumping. Sing "Five Little Speckled Frogs" and encourage the "little frogs" in your classroom to jump as you sing.

Five Little Speckled Frogs
(Directions for older children: Five children sit in a row and the other children sit in a circle around them. All children act out the words to the song.)
Five little speckled frogs (hold up five fingers)
Sitting on a speckled log
Eating some most delicious bug. (pretend to eat bugs)
Yum! Yum!
One jumped into the pool, (one child from center jumps back into the circle)
Where it was nice and cool. (cross arms over chest and shiver)
Now there are four little speckled frogs.
Burr-ump!

Little Mouse. Invite the children to play "Little Mouse" (see page 102).

Outdoor Painting. Give young painters paintbrushes and a pail of water. Encourage them to paint the fence or the building outdoors.

THE COMPLETE RESOURCE BOOK FOR INFANTS

Popcorn Poppers. Encourage babies to pop up and down like popcorn when it's popping. Sing "Popcorn Pop" while the children are popping.

> **Popcorn Pop** by Pam Schiller (Tune: Row, Row, Row Your Boat)
> Pop, pop, pop, popcorn
> Pop it everywhere.
> Poppity, poppity, poppity, poppity.
> Popcorn in the air.
>
> Pop…pop…pop…pop.
> Poppity, poppity, poppity, pop!

Motor Boat. Hold hands with "walkers" and turn in a circle. Say the "Motor Boat" chant as you walk. Start saying it slowly and then increase your walking speed as you say the line "go so fast." With young children you can say the chant without holding hands or walking with others. Let it be an individual activity.

> **Motor Boat**
> Motor boat, motor boat, go so slow. (walk in a circle slowly while chanting)
> Motor boat, motor boat, go so fast. (walk quickly while continuing to chant)

Light Stepping. Shine a flashlight on the floor and invite infants to step on the light. Let them shine the light on the floor and you step on the light. You may want to demonstrate this activity with another adult so that children understand how to do it.

Catch Me If You Can. Chase an infant. Say, *I'm going to get you* and move towards him. Let him get away from you some of the time and then from time to time, catch him. As he grows used to the game and as he approaches 19 months, he will learn how to turn the tables and chase you.

18+ Months

Cat and Mouse. Play a game of Cat and Mouse with children. Say the rhyme below and have the children act it out.

Old Gray Cat
The old gray cat is sleeping, sleeping, sleeping.
The old gray cat is sleeping in the house. (one child is a cat and curls up, pretending to sleep)

The little mice are creeping, creeping, creeping.
The little mice are creeping through the house. (other children are mice creeping around sleeping cat)

The old gray cat is waking, waking, waking.
The old gray cat is waking through the house. (cat slowly sits up and stretches)

The old gray cat is chasing, chasing, chasing.
The old gray cat is chasing through the house. (cat chases mice)

All the mice are squealing, squealing, squealing.
All the mice are squealing through the house. (mice squeal; when the cat catches a mouse, that mouse becomes the cat)

Little Chicks. Encourage the children to play "Little Chicks."

Little Chicks

Little chicks say, "Peep, peep, peep,"
As they wake from sleep, sleep, sleep. (rub eyes)
Little chicks say, "Peep, peep, peep,"
And hear the birds go "cheep, cheep, cheep." (repeat "cheep, cheep, cheep")
Little chicks say, "Peep, peep, peep,"
And watch the chicks leap, leap, leap. (jump up and down)
Little chicks say, "Peep, peep, peep,"
And now it's time to go to sleep. (lay head in hands)

Freeze. Encourage children to dance creatively to music and to stop dancing when the music stops. Show them how to hold a freeze position. Some children will be able to do this activity easily, while others may keep dancing. Some may be able to stop dancing but will not be able to hold their position. This is an activity that will evolve as children mature and as they repeat the activity.

Mr. Wiggle and Mr. Waggle. Tell the babies the story of Mr. Wiggle and Mr. Waggle (appendix page 216). Encourage them to do the hand motions with you. Teach them to add the sound effects of doors closing and opening and of the knocking sounds.

Ring Toss. Make a simple ring toss game by filling clear plastic one-half liter bottles with sand to create stakes. Cut the center from plastic coffee can lids to make rings. Challenge infants to toss the rings around the bottles.

Front Rolls. Teach infants how to do Front Rolls. Move to an open, carpeted area of the room. Show them how to squat, tuck in their heads and roll. **Safety Note:** Supervise children closely to make sure that no one accidentally kicks someone else or tries to roll in an area where they might get hurt.

Chapter 4

Cognitive Development—
Making Sense of the World

Overview

The first cognitive construct that is wired in the brain is the relationship between cause and effect. For the first year of life, infants will diligently strive to understand what causes things to happen. What brings you to them when they cry? What makes the mobile above them move? What happens if they shake an item in their hand? What causes the lights to go on and off?

By the middle of the second year of life, an infant's cognitive focus will change from cause and effect to problem solving. Babies will want to know how to keep a stack of blocks from tumbling down, how to get a peg in a hole, and how to get from one place to another without stepping on something. All the while, they are driven by curiosity and aided by creativity. In the short span of two years, they will make great strides in unraveling the mysteries and complexities of their experience in the world.

Understanding Cause-and-Effect Relationships

Infants need to learn about the world in which they live. The understanding of cause and effect is one of the first cognitive and social-emotional concepts a baby learns.

According to Craig and Sharon Ramey, "for normal growth and development, young infants right from birth need to learn that they can cause good things to happen on a predictable basis" (Ramey and Ramey, 1999 p. 45). Babies need to understand that what happens to them depends on what they do. For example, very early in life babies will learn how to get your attention. A smile will cause you to smile. Cooing will bring a response from you. Crying will bring you to them. This is a natural give and take between a baby and the world (Ramey and Ramey, 1999).

The research of Craig and Sharon Ramey (1999) shows that infants reap the following benefits when they have positive "cause and effect" (response-contingent) experiences in their world, including:

- Increased alertness and more vigorous activity levels,
- Spontaneous expressions of delight and surprise,
- Increased and more diverse vocalization,
- Increased attention to external stimuli,
- More interest in what their own bodies can do,
- Frequent signs of glee and joy, and
- Higher awareness of their own sensory motor capabilities.

Babies learn cause-and-effect relationships by experiencing cause-and-effect activities and happenings. People are the greatest source of these experiences. Toward the end of the first year of life, when babies become more active in their exploration, they will extend their understanding of cause and effect to the greater world.

Early causal experiences need to provide immediate effect for the baby to make the connection. Once babies understand the basic relationship, the time span between cause and effect can be more prolonged.

Problem Solving

Infants are born curious and capable of generating solutions to problems. Everyone has seen a baby who is intent on reaching a toy try various strategies until she gets what she wants. Every parent has experienced the endless maneuvers of a child trying to secure adult attention.

If the natural curiosity of infants is supported by the adults they encounter, they will continue to use creativity and imagination in their approach to daily experiences. If it is stifled, they will become dependent on adult approval and less likely to have enough confidence to forge ahead alone. The critical steps involved in trial-and-error learning begin to be extinguished.

Classroom activities need to stimulate infant's natural ability to think critically and creatively. Caregivers need to model problem-solving strategies and discuss their thinking as they work through problems.

Following are the typical steps to solving problems. It is a natural process, but infants are novices in this area. They will need to practice these skills so they can internalize the problem-solving process.

- Step 1—Identify the problem, for example, the ball has rolled under the bed where I cannot reach and I still want to play with it.
- Step 2—Generate solutions to the problem, for example, move the bed, use a stick to dislodge the ball, roll in another ball to dislodge the ball, get an adult to help, and so on.
- Step 3—Select one of the solutions, for example, get a stick.
- Step 4—Test my choice, for example, try using the stick to reach the ball.
- Step 5—Evaluate the results. Did it work? Was it the best solution? Is the problem solved permanently or just temporarily?

Pay attention to opportunities to let babies solve their own problems. Letting them develop problem-solving skills is one of the best gifts you can give them.

Curiosity

Infants are born with curiosity. They have a reverence for everything and a profound drive to explore and discover. It is curiosity that uncovers the relationship between cause and effect, the joy of using imagination, the pride that accompanies creativity, and the self-confidence that blooms with solving problems.

Creativity

Creativity is defined as the ability to come up with something new—to express individual perspective—to express one's inner self. Although creativity may be part of, and certainly enhances, problem solving, it is different from problem solving.

Creativity develops as infants become grounded in the understanding of cause-and-effect relationships, as language develops, and as motor control improves. It flourishes as infants become more proficient in the self-expression aspect of both language and movement.

Newborns have no reference for creative thought and no motor control to be able to express it. Thoughtful self-expression does not begin until around eight months, and even then it is primitive compared to what a baby can think of and do at around 15 months when her sense of self emerges (Ramey and Ramey, 1999). All infants are born creative, and as they grow and develop their creative expressions will emerge. Some will be more creative than others, but they will all express themselves creatively.

Although creativity is not present at birth and develops only with maturity, it can still be nourished right from birth. In the classroom, encourage creativity throughout the day in almost everything that infants do. Specifically, three learning areas that offer particularly fertile opportunities to encourage infant's creative efforts include art, blocks, and dramatic play. Letting infants explore artistic mediums, providing opportunities for building, and providing props for dramatic play are easy ways to get creativity flowing in the infant classroom.

Experiences and Activities to Explore

Cause-and-Effect Relationships

Birth–18+ Months

Cause-and-Effect Words to Know. Teach infants vocabulary words related to cause and effect. Use the words in the chart below when appropriate and as often as you can with babies.

Cause-and-Effect Books. Read books with cause-and-effect themes. Here are a few

Bounce	Fall	Open	Shake
Break	Happy	Out	Shut
Cause	In	Play	Smile
Clap	Laugh	Pull	Spin
Close	Light	Push	Tap
Crank	Like	Response	Turn
Cry	Move	Ring	Up
Dislike	Off	Roll	
Down	On	Sad	

favorites:

> *Baby Faces* by Margaret Miller
> *Bounce Bounce Bounce* by Kathy Henderson
> *Clap Hands* by Helen Oxenbury
> *If You Give a Mouse a Cookie* by Laura Joffe Numeroff
> *What Makes Me Happy?* by Catherine and Laurence Anholt

Games That Make Me Laugh. Play cause-and-effect games that make infants laugh, such as Peek-a-Boo, Washington Square, 'Round the House, and Pat-a-Cake (appendix page 210).

Washington Square
From here to there (begin tracing a square)
To Washington Square.
When I get near
I'll kiss your hair. (gently kiss the child's hair)
'Round the House
'Round the house, (use index finger to trace a circle on the child's open palm)

'Round the house,

Goes the little mousie.

Up the stairs, (walk index finger and middle finger up the child's arm)

Up the stairs,

In her little housie. (tickle the child under her arm or under her chin.)

Returning Smiles. When a baby smiles, comment about her beautiful smile and give her a great big smile back. Smiling is a great cause-and-effect activity. You can make someone smile with your smile.

Hello and Goodbye. Make sure that you greet babies each day. They will learn to connect hello with seeing you at the beginning of a new day. Say goodbye when a baby leaves and she will learn that leaving prompts a goodbye response. Sing, "Now It's Time to Say Goodbye" (see appendix page 193).

Birth–6 Months

Exaggerated Responses. Make exaggerated responses to an infant's first smiles and vocalizations.

Music Overhead. Provide musical mobiles. Tell the baby that you are starting the mobile by winding it or by turning it on. **Safety Note:** Keep all mobiles out of the reach of infants.

Baby Bells. Make Baby Bells (appendix page 224) for infants. Securely sew a few jingle bells to a child-size scrunchie that fits loosely around a baby's wrists and ankles. When the baby moves, the bell will jingle. You can get the same effect by sewing bells on the baby's socks. **Safety Note:** Supervise closely to make sure the bells do not come loose from the scrunchie or socks.

Rattles. Provide a variety of rattles that produce different sounds. Help infants associate their movements with the sounds of the rattles. As they get older, show them how to make distinct sounds by creating an auditory pattern with the rattle, for example, shake-shake-pause, shake-shake-pause.

Pulley Bag. Attach a Pulley Bag (appendix page 232) to a baby's ankle. Can she figure

out how to make it move up and down?

Tumbling Towers. Lay a baby on her tummy. Place a small tower of two or three Paper Bag Blocks (appendix page 232) in front of her. Invite her to knock the tower down. She may have her own ideas about how to interact with the structure. Follow her lead.

Puffs of Air. Use a baster to blow little puffs of air on a baby's hands and feet. Talk to her about the relationship between pressing the baster bulb and the puff of air.

Off and On. Stand with a baby by a light fixture and show her how to turn it *off* and *on*.

Wiggle the Mobile. Wiggle a mobile over a baby's head. Show her how to kick her feet to wiggle her mobile. Does she make the connection between her legs kicking and the mobile wiggling? After a few kicks, she should see that her kicking shakes the crib. Keep this activity short. Infants belong out of the crib when they are awake.

Stick Out Your Tongue. Stick your tongue out at a baby. Babies read facial features well, and in no time at all, you will be rewarded with the baby sticking out her tongue in response.

With Just a Little Help. Place a "beginning scooter" on her stomach on a blanket. Hold your hands against the bottoms of her feet. When she pushes, hold your hands firmly. She will move forward. Does she understand that her pushing is moving her? You might want to place a favorite toy a few inches in front of her as an incentive to move.

6–12 Months

Cause-and-Effect Toys. Provide age-appropriate toys that are based on cause-and-effect relationships like rattles, Jack-in-the-Boxes, music boxes, and Busy Boxes.

Mimicking Games. Mimic babies' actions. When they clap, you clap. When they smile, you smile. When they babble, you babble back.

Rattle Retrieval. Tie a rattle to one end of a piece of yarn. Tie the other end of the yarn to a baby's highchair. She will love tossing the rattle over the side of the chair and then retrieving it. This will also save you the effort of playing retriever.

Sound Shakers. Make Sound Shakers (appendix page 233) from film canisters (just the right size for holding with little hands). Fill the canisters with interesting sound-making items such as jingle bells, pennies, and buttons. Glue the lids on securely. As babies get older they will learn that the harder they shake, the louder the sound. **Safety Note:** Supervise closely to make sure the lid stays on the container.

Bottle Rollers. Make several Bottle Rollers (appendix page 225). Give babies the bottles and encourage them to roll the bottles across the floor. *What happens to the items inside?*

Through the Tunnel. Drape a sheet over a rectangular table to create a tunnel. Place a special toy at one end of the tunnel. Who crawls through to get the toy?

One, Two, Three. When picking a baby up give a signal. Say, "One, two, three, up you go!" Baby will learn to anticipate the lift.

Calling All Drummers. Give infants cardboard boxes and a cardboard drumstick (cardboard tube from a coat hanger). Invite the drummers to drum away.

Ring, Beep, Blink. Invite children to play with toys that make sounds or light up when buttons are pressed or knobs are turned, such as a music cube or toy telephone.

What Moves the Bubbles? Blow bubbles where a baby can see them. Ask another adult to blow the bubbles gently back toward the baby. *What makes the bubbles change direction?*

12–18+ Months

How Do These Work? Bring in a large colorful shopping bag tied with a big bow. Fill it with items you can use to demonstrate cause-and-effect relationships, for example, a music box, a flashlight, a doll or stuffed animal that speaks when squeezed, a service bell, a battery-operated radio, and so on. Demonstrate the "cause" of each item's action and teach the associated vocabulary; wind, turn on, squeeze, and so on.

THE COMPLETE RESOURCE BOOK FOR INFANTS

Shadow Dancing. Stand babies between a light source and a wall and encourage them to dance. Point out that their bodies are blocking out the light.

Shadow Puppets. Make shadow puppets on the wall. Help infants see that the interruption of light by your hands creates the shadows.

Sunny Day Shadows. Show infants their shadows on a sunny day. Show them how to make their shadow grow taller and shorter.

Flashlight Fun. Allow infants to explore a flashlight. Show them how to turn it off and on. Demonstrate moving the light around the room. Show the infants how the classroom's light turns off and on.

Ring That Bell. Obtain a service bell. Show older babies how to toss a beanbag to ring the bell.

Jump and Light Shoes. When older babies wear a pair of shoes that light up when they walk, call attention to how jumping and moving turns on the light. Show the infants different ways to make the lights on their shoes work, including tapping their shoes together, tapping their shoes on a table leg, or tapping their shoes with their hands.

Putty in My Hands. Give infants playdough. Talk about how you can smash it, roll it, and punch it.

Rum Tum Tum. Give the infants drums to play (appendix page 227). As the drummers drum, talk with them about the sounds they are making. Point out the relationship between the force of their hit and the resulting sound. Suggest making loud sounds. Suggest making soft sounds. Do the drummers see the cause-and-effect relationship? They will in time.

Sound Makers. Provide a variety of sound makers, for example, jingle bells, clappers, drums, rattles, music boxes, and so on. Encourage the infants to explore what causes each item to make sounds.

Colored Glasses. Gather pairs of old sunglasses and regular glasses. Remove all of the lenses and cover the frames with colored cellophane where the lenses used to be. Invite the infants to look through the glasses. Describe what happens. **Safety Note:** Be sure that the cellophane is securely attached to the glasses and that infants do not put pieces of cellophane in their mouths.

Beach Ball Batting. Suspend a beach ball from the ceiling at a height that is just above the infant's heads but not so high that they can't reach it. Demonstrate how batting the ball with your hands moves it. *If you hit the ball harder will it move faster? Will it move further? Can you make the ball move in a circle?*

Downhill Run. Create an inclined plane. Give the infants small cars to run up and down the "hill." Talk with the infants about the difference between pushing their cars up the hill and allowing them to run freely down the hill. Talk about what makes the trip down so easy and so fast.

Spinning Tops. Spin tops for babies to watch. Talk with them about spinning. Show them the point of the top and explain that the top has no "feet" to stand on. When the top is not spinning, it falls down. Encourage babies to spin like tops and drop to the floor when they are through spinning. Make sure you are on a carpeted area and that you supervise the spinning so that babies don't get dizzy and fall unintentionally.

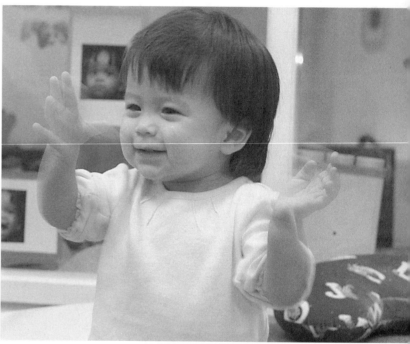

Tall Towers Falling Down. Invite the infants to stack the Paper Bag Blocks (appendix page 232). Show infants how the blocks can be knocked down with their hands, their heads, or with a beanbag.

Musical Toys. Provide a variety of musical toys with a variety of types of music and a variety of mechanisms for turning them on and off.

Bowling. Make Bowling Pins (appendix page 225). Give the infants a small, soft ball to use to knock the pins down. Talk with them as they play. Talk with them about what makes the pins fall. *Do more pins fall when the ball is thrown hard or when the ball is thrown gently? Does the game work if the ball is kicked instead of thrown?*

Spinning Face. Make a Spinning Face (appendix page 233). Suspend the Spinning Face. Invite babies to toss a beanbag to spin the spinning face. Talk with infants about what makes the face spin.

Red and Yellow Make Orange. Put a small amount of yellow fingerpaint on one of the infant's hands and red fingerpaint on the other hand. Show her how to rub her hands together to create orange. Provide paper and encourage her to create an orange picture.

Color Surprises. Place a small amount of blue paint and mild detergent in the water in the water play table. After a few minutes, add a small amount of yellow paint. Encourage the infants to move the water to mix the colors. Say, *When one color mixes with another color, the color changes.* It is not important for infants to know which two colors can be mixed to create a third color.

Spinning Tops. Spin tops for children. Older infants may figure out how to spin the top by themselves.

18+ Months

Hand Warmer. Show the infants how to rub their hands together to keep them warm. Say, *Rubbing things together creates warmth. When we rub our hands together we help them stay warm.*

Writing Tools. Give the infants crayons, chalk, pencils, and markers. As they explore each tool, discuss the different types of marks each tool creates. *How do the tools move differently on the paper? Which marks are darkest? Which mark is the lightest? Which tool do you like best?*

Playdough Molders. Mix a batch of playdough (appendix pages 222–223). Show the infants several ways to flatten a ball of dough, for example, using a rolling pin, patting it between their hands, and pressing it with a book. *What happens when you pinch the dough? What happens when you roll the dough? What happens when you pull the dough?*

Magic Mover. Place small metal objects inside an empty, plastic two-liter bottle. Seal the lid securely. Give the infants a large horseshoe magnet and show them how to move the items inside the bottle with the magnet. Show the infants how the magnet sticks to other metal things in the room.

Paper Fan Breeze. Make paper fans for the infants and show them how to create a breeze. Say, *We can move the air with a fan. We can feel the air when it moves.*

Back Thing! Make yourself a Magic Wand (appendix page 231) out of a cardboard insert from a coat hanger. Encourage the infants to chase you. Teach them to back away when you hold out your wand and say, "Back, Thing!" (appendix page 217).

Experiences and Activities to Practice Problem-Solving Skills

Birth–18+ Months

Problem-Solving Words to Know. Teach infants vocabulary words related to problem-solving skills. Use the words in the chart below when appropriate and as often as you can.

Choices	Determined	Problem	Think
Creative	Imagination	Solution	Try
Decision	Persistent	Test	Wonder

Books About Problem Solving. Read books that promote problem solving and thinking. Here are some favorites:

Five Little Monkeys With Nothing to Do by Eileen Christelow
Hush Little Baby by Sylvia Long
Itsy Bitsy Spider by Iza Trapani

Self-Talk. As you encounter problems during the day, talk about the possible solutions and then verbalize your choice of solutions. If you solve the problem, let the infants know about your success. Infants can't see the process of problem solving inside your head. Verbalizing the steps to solving problems helps infants understand how solutions are achieved.

Let Them Do It. When child-size problems arise in the classroom, encourage infants to solve them. Often, it is easier to solve them yourself but, in doing so you are denying infants the opportunity to practice problem-solving skills. Thinking skills are wired in the brain between birth and age four. Wiring requires opportunities to experience the problem-solving process. Strong wiring requires repetition and lots of practice.

Birth–6 Months

Get It. Place a small colorful toy on one end of a towel and the other end of the towel close to a baby. Does she figure out that the toy can be brought closer by pulling the towel? If she gets frustrated, hand her the toy.

Roll Over. Learning to roll over is a major feat for babies, and they need practice to learn how to do it. When a baby seems ready to roll over, assist her by sitting down beside her and gently pulling the leg that is on the opposite side of where you are sitting.

Out of Reach. Place the baby on her tummy and put a desired toy just out of her reach. See if she will try to wiggle to move herself toward the toy. If she gets frustrated, move the toy closer.

Tactile Mountains. Place several textured pillows on the floor for baby to crawl over. Can she make it to her destination? Sing "The Bear Went Over the Mountain," substituting her name for the bear. Use action and position words like *climbing, over, under, down,* and *pulling* to describe infant's movements.

Baby Talk. Talk to a baby about the many ways you know what she wants or needs. *I can tell when you are hungry because you get fussy. I can tell when you have a gas pain because you let out a cry and kick your legs. I can tell when you are wet because you get fidgety.*

Grab the Ring. Tie one end of a ribbon to a small toy and the other end to an embroidery hoop. Place the hoop just out of babies reach. Encourage her to scoot toward the ring and pull it to get the toy. Demonstrate how this works so baby will see what to do.

Reaching. Place a favorite toy just out of reach and encourage baby to reach for it. Say encouraging words to her as she struggles toward her goal. You're going to get it. You're getting closer. You're almost there. Stretch. Give her a "thumbs up" when she achieves her goal.

Talk the Talk. Highlight problem-solving situations with the appropriate language. *How are you going to get that? How can you see that better? Can you make the mobile move?*

Come and Get It. Place two or three rattles at the edge of a blanket. Place baby on the opposite edge of the blanket. Shake the rattles to encourage baby to scoot, roll, or crawl to get the noisemakers.

Problem-Solving Toys. Provide toys that encourage problem solving, such as stacking rings, sorting boxes, nesting cubes, and one-piece puzzles. Encourage babies to explore the toys. Assist them in discovering how each toy works.

6–12 Months

Two Hands, Three Toys. Offer a third toy to a child who is already holding on to two toys. How does she get the third toy in hand?

Hide-and-Seek Bottles. Make a Hide-and-Seek Bottle (appendix page 229) and give it to infants to explore. With time they will figure out that to see the ball again they must turn the bottle over.

Can't Fool Me. Sit down on the floor with the baby. Show her a toy and then hide it under a blanket. Does she pull the blanket away to find the toy? Typically, somewhere between seven and eight months babies will start to look for a hidden item. However, some infants will begin to look for out-of-sight objects sooner.

Toy Overboard. Attach a piece of yarn or learning links to a small toy and to the side of the feeding table. Show babies how to retrieve the toy when it is thrown overboard.

Tactile Path. Place several items, such as bubble wrap, burlap, large buttons, wooden or plastic blocks, a carpet square, and two or three pieces of contact paper sticky side up, on the floor to create a tactile pathway. Take a baby's shoes off and let her crawl or walk the tactile pathway. Can anyone travel on the path without getting stuck? After the infants have explored crawling or walking the path, encourage them to touch the items on the pathway. Talk with them about the various textures of the items.

Boxes and Lids. Provide several different sizes of boxes with lids. Challenge babies to find the correct lid for each box. What strategies do they use?

Amazing Mazes. Create a maze with pillows, chairs, boxes, and so on. Challenge your crawlers to crawl through the maze.

Shake, Shake, Shake. Cut a hole in the top of a shoebox or similar type of box. Tape the lid on securely. Place a ball in the box. Encourage babies to figure how to get the ball out of the box.

Mitten Interference. Collect pairs of mittens and gloves. Let the infants wear the mittens while they are playing. Do the mittens get in the way? Do the infants find it difficult to pick up items with the mittens on? Watch carefully to make sure that none of the infants are becoming frustrated with the mittens. Does anyone take the mittens off?

Shoe Match. Give babies shoes to match. Talk with them as they find the matching pairs. How do they know which shoes go together?

Lightest to Darkest. Give infants several shades of the same color of 4" x 4" construction paper squares. Help them arrange the squares from lightest to darkest shades. This is an important task because during the first two years of life the eye becomes trained to recognize and categorize colors.

Which Toy? Which Box? Hide two different toys under two identical medium-size boxes. Show infants the toys and let them watch you place the toys under the boxes. Move the boxes around. Ask the infants which toy is under which box.

12–18+ Months

Simple Puzzles. Provide one-piece simple puzzles for babies to solve. Talk with them as they work. Demonstrate turning the puzzle piece to get it to fit.

Little Construction Workers. Build with babies. With practice, she will learn how to keep the building from falling, how to pick just the right size block to fill a gap, and to build more elaborate structures.

Nesting Boxes. Give the infant three or four boxes of graduated sizes. Help her discover that the boxes fit inside one another. Do some infants figure it out by themselves?

Come on Through. Attach a 2' piece of yarn or string (or learning links) to a small car and then run the other end of the yarn or string through an empty paper towel tube. Show infants how to pull the car through the "tunnel."

Heart Hunt. During naptime, place several construction paper hearts around the room. Hang some on the wall at children's eye level. Hide some in the toy area. Place some by the changing table. When infants wake up, show them a heart and invite them to find the others.

Sandbox Treasures. Place ping-pong balls or large buttons in a small tub of sand. Provide strainers and show the infants how to scoop the sand and sift to find a treasure. Place the tub on a shower curtain liner or old tablecloth to make cleanup easier.

Setting the Stage. When infants get into squabbles, intercede with words that help them build a foundation for conflict resolution. *Steve, Richele has the ball right now. Let's see if you can find another toy. Richele, when you finish playing with the ball will you let Steve know?* You will be surprised by how quickly babies catch on. In no time at all, Richele will take the ball to Steve when she is finished.

Choices. Offer infants choices as often as possible. Making choices is an important part of problem solving.

High Hopes. Suspend a beach ball from the ceiling just barely out of reach of the infants. Provide empty paper towel tubes, folded papers, stuffed animals, and anything else that can be used to touch the beach ball. Challenge the infants to think of ways to touch the ball.

Can You Do This? Build a simple structure with the blocks. Ask the infants to copy your structure.

Bubbles Up. Blow bubbles for the infants. Challenge them to keep the bubbles from landing on the ground. Offer suggestions about how they might keep the bubbles up.

Things That Go Together. Give the infants pairs of shoes, mittens, and socks to match.

Upside Down Cup. Turn a cup upside down on the baby's feeding tray. Can she turn it right side up?

Fix the Face. Construct a face using felt cutouts on the flannel board. Leave off a feature, such as a nose or an eye, and ask the baby to fix the face.

Problem-Solving Language. When infants encounter a problem, use the language of problem-solving to help them work through it. Ask questions to encourage exploration. *It looks like you have a problem. How will you solve it? There is always more than one solution. What can you do?*

18+ Months

Puzzle Fun. Provide puzzles for infants to work. You can make simple and interesting puzzles by cutting the front of a cereal box or greeting card into puzzle pieces.

Cleanup Helper. When infants spill something, let them help you clean it up. Show them how to use a sponge, a rag, and a napkin. Help them decide which item works best.

Thinking About Solutions. When a ball rolls under the chair, ask infants to think of a way to get it. If you are helping the infants find a solution, describe each step of your thinking.

Coat or No Coat. Let infants help decide whether or not they need a coat when going outdoors. Model ways to ensure you are making a good choice, such as looking out the window and feeling the windowpane to determine if the wind is blowing or if the air is chilly.

Separating Solids. Place rocks and sand in a tub. Give infants a strainer and two containers. Challenge them to separate the rocks from the sand.

Experiences and Activities to Promote Curiosity

Birth–18+ Months

Curiosity Words to Know. Teach infants vocabulary words related to curiosity. Use the words in the chart below when appropriate and as often as you can.

Aroma	How	Look	Taste
Curious	Inquisitive	Notice	Touch
Explore	Interest	Observe	Where
Feel	Investigate	See	Why
Hear	Listen	Smell	Wonder

Books About Wonder and Curiosity. Read books that stimulate curiosity. Here are a few suggestions:

I Touch by Rachal Isadora
Peek-a-Who? by Nina Laden
What's on My Head? by Margaret Miller

Pocket Full of Wonders. Wear an apron with pockets in it. From time to time put treasures, such as a prism, a pinecone, a mirror, a charm bracelet, or any other interesting items in your pockets and take them out to show them during the day.

Wave Machines. Make Wave Machines (appendix page 235) for infants to explore. Assist younger babies by moving the wave machines for them, if necessary. Talk to the infants about the colors in the bottle and the movement of the water.

Colored Reflections. Tape colored cellophane over a mirror. Sit on the floor with a baby on your lap and look at the colored reflection. What make the mirror images look different? Remember that young infants (birth–6 months) are limited as to colors they can recognize. Use red or blue cellophane for young infants. With babies older than six months, you can use any color of cellophane. **Safety Note:** Keep cellophane out of the reach of infants. Be sure they do not put cellophane in their mouths.

Picture Collection. Keep a collection of interesting pictures in plastic sleeves in a three-ring binder. Encourage babies to look at the pictures. Display special pictures on the wall for babies to look at.

Colored Streamers. Hang colored streamers over the changing table. Young infants will watch the streamers move with the air. Talk with older infants about the colors of the streamers and what moves them.

Pinwheels. Make or buy pinwheels for infants to explore. Encourage them to take the pinwheels outdoors and run with them. Show the infants how to blow the pinwheels. Place pinwheels on feeding tables and direct a fan on them to make them move. **Safety Note:** Supervise closely, especially if infants are running with pinwheels. Make sure that the sticks attached to the pinwheels are soft. If you make the pinwheel, use a straw as a stick.

New Discoveries. Watch as infants make new discoveries today. Take time to talk with them about their new awareness. For example, one child might discover her hands, while another might try spinach for the first time. Still others may learn to move something on the busy box. All new discoveries are the result of experimentation.

Tie a Yellow Ribbon. Tie bright yellow (or any bright color) textured ribbon around a baby's bottle. Does she notice the color? Place her hands on the ribbon so she can feel the new addition to her bottle. Talk to her about the ribbon's color and texture. **Safety Note:** Remove the ribbon from the bottle and put it away after baby has finished eating.

Birth–6 Months

Sock Rattle. Place a sock over a rattle and tape it closed with masking tape. Give the rattle to an infant and let her explore it. After a little while, take the sock off the rattle and let her play with it again.

See and Burp. Use a brightly colored patterned towel as a burping towel to create a change of scenery for baby. Talk to her about the colors and patterns in the towel.

Gel Bags. Fill a plastic resealable bag with hair gel. Tape the bag closed. Give the bag to baby and let her play with it. Encourage her to squeeze the bag. **Safety Note:** Supervise closely so the baby does not put the plastic bag in her mouth.

Colored Lights. Place a string of colored lights in an area within infants' view but out of reach. Arrange the light colors in a pattern, such as red, yellow, red, yellow. Describe the lights to them using descriptive language.

Balloon Watch. Attach a Mylar balloon above the changing table. Babies will love watching it float back and forth above them.

A Change of View. When feeding a baby her bottle, change directions or locations once in a while. Move your chair or hold the baby with her head resting on your left arm instead of your right. Change the end of the crib you use when you lay baby down for a nap. A change of view is good for everyone.

Mobile Rotation. Change mobiles in the classroom often. You can rotate them if they are different. If mobiles are all alike and you do not have additional mobiles to exchange for existing mobiles, add ribbons and bows or other new items to the mobile. Babies will love to see the new items. **Safety Note:** Be sure mobiles are always out of the reach of infants.

Color Matters. Provide brightly colored toys for infants. A baby will learn to recognize the color red some time around the third month but can only learn what she has experienced. The next colors she will recognize are blue and green. Provide lots of opportunity for babies to experience colors.

A Look From Here and a Look From There. Show a baby a large item, such as a stuffed animal, a top, a stack of blocks, and so on. Take a close look at the item and describe to the baby the visible characteristics of the item. With babies who are at least a month old, walk a few feet away from the item and look at it again. Describe what you see from this distance. With babies who are three months old and older, walk across the room and take another look.

From All Angles. Place a baby on her stomach on the floor. Place a large stuffed animal close by but out of her reach. After she looks at the stuffed animal for a while, turn it one-quarter rotation and encourage baby to look at the animal again. Continue rotating until the animal has made a full turn. This activity will help baby develop her visual perception.

Busy Box Changes. Turn busy boxes upside down. What do infants think about this new perspective?

Spectators. Hold babies in your lap so they can watch the older infants as they play Partner Ball Play (appendix page 218).

Sticky Ball. Make a Sticky Ball (appendix page 234) and give it to babies to explore.

Facial Perspectives. Let infants view your face from different perspectives. Hold a baby up over your head and raise and lower her so that she can see your face up close and at a distance.

6–12 Months

Everything the Same Color. During playtime, collect toys that are all the same color and place them around the infants. Talk about the color.

A New View. Move babies' highchairs from time to time. A new view is inspiring to everyone and novelty helps hold infants' attention.

Tactile Blocks. Make a set of Tactile Blocks (appendix page 234). Encourage infants to explore the blocks as they build or stack. Talk about the textures. *This block feels smooth, but this block feels scratchy. Feel this smooth one with your hands. How does it feel? How does it feel on your face? Which block feels the nicest?* Work with infants to find the roughest texture and the smoothest texture. Assist young builders in ordering the blocks from roughest to smoothest.

Keep Your Eye on the Ball. Get a baby's attention. Roll a ball across the room. Say, *Keep your eyes on the ball. Where is it going?* Infants six months and older should be able to easily follow the movement of the ball.

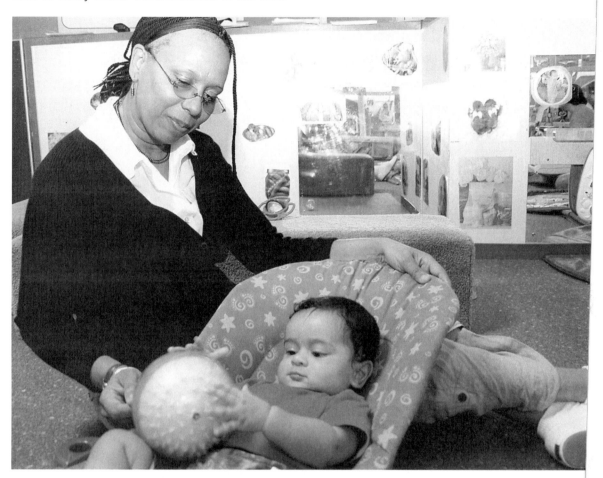

In and Out. Give infants ping-pong balls and a cardboard tube approximately 3" in diameter. Potato chip cans work well if you remove the bottom. Show babies how to drop the balls through the tube.

Dippety Do Dots. Fill a plastic bottle with hair gel and then add colorful sequins. Invite young explorers to roll the bottles and watch the floating sequin "dots."

Aroma Puffs. Dab different massage oils sparsely on a powder puff or cotton ball. Sit with infants and let them smell the puffs. Do babies seem to favor one scent over another?

Food Smells. Invite babies to smell their food before eating it. Talk about the various smells.

Purses and Billfolds. Collect old purses and billfolds. Fill them with items of interest that are both safe and fun to manipulate, such as expired credit cards, plastic mirrors, combs, and any other objects that are safe for babies. Give the purses and billfolds to infants to explore. Talk with them about the things they find inside.

Where's Charlie? Hide a small stuffed animal under a plastic cup. Say, *Where's Charlie?* Call Charlie's name a couple of times. Take the cup away and say, *There he is!* Play the Hide and Seek game a few times. You may want to change the name of the animal you hide each time. Hand the cup and the animal to the baby and let her play the game by herself.

Comparisons. Place a photo of an object and the real object side by side for a baby to look at. Talk with the baby about what she sees. Have her touch both the picture and the real object.

Baggie Ice Cream. Invite babies to help you make Baggie Ice Cream (appendix page 219). You will have a lot of help! Talk with your helpers about the ingredients in the ice cream. Talk with them about how the ice cream tastes and how it feels. Is it cold? Do you like the flavor? Recite the "Ice Cream Chant" (appendix page 208) while infants enjoy their ice cream. **Safety Note:** Check for allergies before serving ice cream.

Peep Hole. Cut a small hole in a paper plate and invite babies to look through the hole.

6–18+ Months

Color Bottle. Make several Color Bottles. Follow the directions for Observation Bottles on appendix page 231, but use only one color for each bottle. Give the bottles to babies to explore. Talk with babies as they play with the bottles. *Which color do you like best? Can you find something else that is the same color as the water in the bottle?*

Ball Chute. Make a Ball Chute (appendix page 224). Encourage young investigators to drop a ball into the chute. Ask questions. *Where does the ball go? Where will it come out?*

Colorscopes. Give the infants Colorscopes (appendix page 226) to explore. Talk with them about what they see.

Color Hoops. Give the infants Color Hoops (appendix page 226) to explore. Ask them questions as they look through the hoops. *What do you see? Do you like the way things look through the hoop?*

12–18+ Months

Eyes in a Bottle. Fill an empty, clear plastic bottle with wiggle eyes. Glue the lid on the bottle and invite babies to explore the bottle.

Rose-Colored Glasses. Give the infants Colored Glasses (appendix page 226) to explore. Talk with them about how the world looks through colored glasses.

Under the Table Art. Tape pictures on the underside of a table and invite babies to crawl under the table and lie on their backs to look at the pictures.

Sniff, Sniff. Hide an Aroma Bag (appendix page 224) and challenge the infants to find it using only their "sniffer" (nose). **Safety Note:** Check for allergies before allowing infants to participate in this activity.

Magnetic Animals and Letters. Give the infants large magnetic toys to stick on a cookie sheet. If you don't have magnetic toys use refrigerator magnets. **Safety Note:** Supervise closely. Be sure infants don't put magnetic toys in their mouths.

Magnet Bottle. Make a Magnet Bottle (appendix page 231). Invite infants to see what they can uncover in the bottle.

Tactile Playdough. Give the infants Tactile Playdough (appendix page 223) to explore. Talk with them about how the playdough feels. *Is it smooth? Is it rough? Is it cool? Is it hard?*

Peppermint Playdough. Invite babies to play with Scented Playdough (appendix page 223). Encourage them to smell the dough as they shape it into interesting shapes. Watch infants closely so that they do not eat the dough. **Safety Note:** This dough is not edible. Using edible playdough can confuse infants. It is better not to mix messages about what is edible and what is not and that food is for nourishment, not for playing.

Scratch and Sniff. Give the infants paper, paintbrushes, and Scratch and Sniff Paint (appendix page 222) to explore. When the paint is dry, invite infants to scratch it and sniff.

Up Close Look. Give young investigators a magnifying glass and some interesting objects such as pinecones, oranges, pieces of fabric, or other objects to investigate.

Sticker Fun. Collect stickers from families. Let babies play with the stickers. Provide boxes, paper plates, and paper to use as a surface to apply the stickers.

Floaters. Provide a shallow tub of water and several items that will float on the water, such as margarine tubs, plastic lids, plastic cups, and so on. For extra fun, add ice cubes to the water.

Gel Bags. Make Gel Bags (appendix page 229). Place ½ cup of hair gel in a plastic resealable bag. Glue the bag shut. Show infants how to use their hands, fingers, feet and toes to move the gel around to create designs. *What happens when you squeeze the bag? What happens when you poke the bag with one finger?* **Safety Note:** Supervise closely. Be sure infants do not put the bags in their mouths.

What's Inside? Freeze a small toy inside a block of ice. Place the ice in a bowl and then in a location where infants can observe it melting. Talk with them about what they think is inside the block of ice.

Real Object Match. Give babies pairs of pictures of objects and corresponding real objects. Challenge them to match the pictures to the real objects.

What's Wrong With This Picture? Place two or three posters or photographs on the wall upside down. Does anyone notice?

Sand Play. Provide a shallow tub of sand and some items to enhance infant's play, such as strainers, funnels, cups, and shovels. To make cleanup easier, place the sand tub on top of a vinyl shower curtain.

Can Rollers. Fill four one-pound coffee cans with varying amount of sand, and glue the lids on securely. Encourage young "adventurers" to roll the cans. Which can rolls fastest? Which can rolls slowest?

Observation Bottles. Make Observation Bottles (appendix page 231) for infants. Talk with them about the items in the bottle. If commercially made observation tubes are available, show the infants how to roll them across the floor.

18+ Months

Sand Combs. Give infants Sand Combs (appendix page 232) to explore. Show them how to make patterns in the sand with the combs either at the sand table or outdoors.

Bubble Poppers. Give infants small bubble wrap. Challenge them to pop the bubbles with their fingers. **Safety Note:** Supervise closely. Be sure infants do not put bubble wrap in their mouths.

Colored Shadows. On a sunny day, give each child a piece of colored cellophane to play with outdoors. Talk with infants about the shadows they can make. **Safety Note:** Supervise closely. Be sure infants do not put cellophane in their mouths.

Playdough Mixing. Give infants two different colors of playdough (appendix page 222) and encourage them to mix the colors together by kneading. Ask them what they think will happen when you mix the colors.

Air Sounds. Provide a bicycle pump. Help the infants experiment with making different sounds by placing the valve of the pump inside an empty plastic bottle and then pumping. *What kind of sound does the air make?* Place the valve inside a small cardboard box and then pump again. *How does the sound change?* Try placing the valve inside other items, such as a paper bag, purse, plastic cup, and so on.

In the Bag. Glue a magazine picture in the bottom of a paper bag. Give a curious child a flashlight and invite her to look into the bag. Ask questions. *What do you see? What's in the bag? May I see what's in the bag?*

Experiences and Activities to Promote Creativity

6–18+ Months

Creativity Words to Know. Teach infants vocabulary words related to creativity. Use the words in the chart below when appropriate and as often as you can.

Build	Crayon	Imagination	Paint
Collage	Create	Imagine	Print
Color	Creation	Make	
Construct	Draw	Model	

Books That Promote Creativity. Read books that promote creative concepts, such as the following:

I Love Colors by Margaret Miller
Red, Blue, Yellow Shoe by Tana Hoban

Rhythm Band. Give older infants rhythm band instruments—younger infants can hold their rattles. Play some lively music and encourage babies to play along.

Creative Opportunities. Keep art materials, building materials, and dress-up clothing readily available. If you are not able to keep them on a low shelf, keep them in a place where you can easily access them when an opportunity for exploration arises.

Art Show. Invite a class of older infants to create art for the infant room.

Art Wall. Place a couple of sheets of poster board together to make a large art area on the wall. Attach a colored pencil to a string and attach the string to the wall by the poster board. Allow infants to draw when the mood strikes.

Birth–6 Months

From birth to six months of age, babies are incapable of creative expression. They have not yet developed the motor control or the conceptual framework to demonstrate creative thought. For these first few months, caretakers need to focus on activities that support the understanding of cause-and-effect and motor development. As babies become more familiar with their surroundings and are in better control of their bodies, they will begin to show an interest in creative activities.

6–12 Months

Peek-a-Boo Art Appreciation. Play Peek-a-Boo using artwork by an older child as a hiding spot instead of your hands, hiding your face behind the piece of artwork.

Art in a Bottle. Obtain deodorant bottles that have snap-on, roller-ball, plastic caps. When the bottles are empty, clean them well and fill them with tempera paint. Give young artists paper and paint-filled deodorant bottles and encourage them to paint.

Box Fun. Give infants several sizes of cardboard boxes. See what they do with the boxes.

Paper Bag Blocks. Encourage young builders to make a creative tower with Paper Bag Blocks (appendix page 232). Talk with them as they build. *How high do you think your tower will be?*

Easy Stick Art. Give infants a sheet of clear contact paper with the sticky side up. Provide torn pieces of tissue paper and invite the infants to select pieces of tissue paper and stick them on their paper.

Necklaces. Help babies string beads or hook colorful links together to make a necklace. Talk about the designs you make and how the pretty colors make the necklace interesting.

Glue Drop Design. Place colored glue in squeeze bottles and encourage young artists to make glue drop designs on drawing paper or construction paper. Talk with them about the colors of the glue drops. **Safety Note:** Supervise closely to ensure that glue goes on the paper and not in the children's mouths.

Fun in a Bag. Give young artists Design Bags (appendix page 227). Encourage them to make a design, erase it, and design again. **Safety Note:** Supervise closely. Be sure that infants don't put bags in their mouths.

Ball Track Designs. Place a sheet of drawing paper inside a box or a cake pan that is 2" deep. Dip a golf ball in tempera paint and place it inside the box or pan. Encourage young painters to roll the ball in the box to create ball track designs.

Fingerpainting. Give the infants fingerpaint and a sheet of fingerpaint paper. As they explore the paint, talk about the feel of the paint on their hands. Use descriptive words, such as gooey, sticky, slimy, and so on. Talk about the color of the paint and how they are covering their entire paper with paint. **Safety Note:** Supervise closely. Be sure infants don't put paint in their eyes or mouths.

Scribbling. Cover a small table or individual feeding chairs with butcher paper. Give babies crayons and encourage them to draw and scribble. Hang individual drawings and/or the group mural in a prominent place so infants and others can appreciate their work.

12–18+ Months

THE COMPLETE RESOURCE BOOK FOR INFANTS

Bubble Creations. Put a few drops of food coloring in bubble solution and encourage infants to blow bubbles over a long strip of bulletin board paper. When the bubbles pop they will make a colored splash. Hang the mural in an area where everyone can see it.

Cookie Cutter Prints. Provide cookie cutters, art paper, and tempera paint. Pour the paint in a shallow tray. Demonstrate placing the cookie cutter in the paint and then on the art paper to make prints. Encourage the young artists to make prints on their paper. Talk with them about the shapes of the cookie cutter and the colors of the paints. Ask questions. Name the shapes they are printing.

Sponge Painting. Cut sponges into geometric shapes. Provide a tray of tempera paint. Attach a clothespin to each sponge to use as a handle. Encourage young artists to dab away. As children work, talk with them about the shapes of the sponges. Describe what they are doing. *You are making a print on your paper with a sponge.*

Textured Fingerpaint. Add salt or sand to fingerpaint (fingerpaint recipe, appendix pages 220–221) and encourage infants to paint directly on a tabletop. Talk with them as they play with the paint. *Fingerpaint is smooth and easy to move around the tabletop, but there is something else in the paint that is not smooth. It is called sand and it makes the paint feel gritty. Do you feel it on your hands?* **Safety Note:** Supervise closely. Be sure that infants don't put paint in their eyes or mouths.

Colorful Blocks. Provide colorful, soft building blocks. Encourage infants to stack them creatively.

Fingerprints. Provide fingerpaint (appendix pages 220–221) and fingerpaint paper. Show babies how to make fingerprints on their paper.

Playdough Creations. Mix playdough (appendix page 222). Encourage the young sculptors to create playdough creations.

Draw With Me. Sit at a table and draw a picture with crayons. Do any of the infants join you? Describe your drawing to your drawing partners.

Easel Painting. Provide easel paper and paint, and encourage infants to paint. If you do not have an easel, make a table easel by cutting a diagonal line from the ends of a copy paper box or a box of similar size.

Imagination and a Box. Give the infants several cardboard boxes to play with. Help the infants think of creative ways to use the boxes. They might use a box as a boat or as a hiding place. They might use several boxes to make a train.

A Hose Can Be Most Anything. Give young thinkers a 2' section of a hose or plastic tubing. See what they make of it. Some might see it as a vacuum. Others might use it like a weed eater. You never know what they might do! Encourage infants to tell you about their pretend play.

Fashion Statements. Collect simple accessories, such as boas, hats, scarves, boots, and other items. Invite babies to dress in accessories of their own choosing. Help them put on the accessories. Describe their outfits as they dress. Talk about the colors they are wearing. Name the clothing and accessory items as they add them to their ensemble.

Sticker Fun. Give infants stickers and items to stick the sticker on. They will be happy with stickers that you get in the mail or even dot stickers. They love sticking them on empty paper towel tubes or cardboard boxes. Let their fun and creativity flourish.

Sidewalk Art. On a nice day, take chalk outdoors and invite young artists to draw on the sidewalk. Describe the different chalk colors they are using. Talk with them about the marks they make. *Look, you made a circle.*

Hand Prints. Invite infants to fingerpaint (appendix pages 220–221) directly on the tabletop. When their hands are covered in paint have them press them onto a clean sheet of drawing paper to create handprints. Talk with infants about their hands. *Let's count your fingers—one, two, three, four, five! You have five fingers on this hand. This part of your hand is called your palm. Do you know which finger is your thumb? That's right! This big finger off to one side is your thumb. Is your hand bigger or smaller than mine?* **Safety Note:** Supervise closely. Be sure infants don't put paint in their eyes or mouths.

Collages. Provide glue or paste and drawing paper. Invite infants to make a collage from any of the following items: torn paper, tissue paper, magazine pictures, leaves or other nature items, pieces of fabric, or scraps of wallpaper.

Car Tracks. Place a sponge on a Styrofoam meat tray. Prepare tempera paint and pour it over the sponge. Give infants a car and some art paper. Show them how to run the car across the sponge and then onto their paper to make car tracks. Encourage them to create a design of car tracks.

Color to the Beat. Give babies large sheets of paper and a crayon. Play some music and encourage infants to color to the beat.

Ice Painting. Put food coloring and water in ice trays. When partially frozen, position a craft stick in each section of the tray. When frozen, give the infants ice on a stick to use as a brush and a piece of paper to paint on.

Props. Provide soft rubber animals, cars, houses and so on, as props for dramatic play. Sit on the floor and help build a garage for toy cars or a barn for toy animals. Make Garages (appendix page 229) and Town Props (appendix page 235) to stimulate play.

18+ Months

Blotto. Give infants a piece of folded construction paper. Drop thick blobs of tempera paint on one side of the folded paper. Show babies how to press the paper together to create a "blotto" design.

Spray Paint Creations. Fill a plastic spray bottle with tempera paint and water. Give the infants shape cutouts. Have them lay the cutouts on a piece of art paper and then spray the tempera paint over the paper. Remove the shape when the paint is dry. Talk about the paintings.

Color Diffusion. Give infants large eyedroppers, coffee filters, and colored water (food coloring in water). Show the infants how to drop colored water on the filters to create a colorful masterpiece.

Colored Markers. Give infants colored markers to explore. To make the activity more interesting, use scented markers.

Strange Brushes. Provide tempera paint and a variety of items to use as brushes, such as a feather, toilet paper tube, stick, feather duster, and so on. Encourage young artists to paint with the instrument of their choice. Talk with them about the "brush" they are using. *Is it easy to hold? Do you like what it does with the paint?*

Appendix

Songs

Beautiful Mommy by Pam Schiller (Tune: K-K-K-Katie)
M-m-m-mommy, beautiful mommy,
I love you more and more and more and more.
M-m-m-mommy, beautiful mommy,
You're the only m-m-m-mommy I adore.

Bubbles in the Air (Tune: If You're Happy and You Know It)
Bubbles in the air, in the air.
Bubbles in the air, in the air.
Bubbles in the air, bubbles everywhere.
Bubbles in the air, in the air.

Bubbles way up there, way up there.
Bubbles way up there, way up there.
Stretch and reach them if you can.
Bubbles way up there, way up there.

Bubbles in my hair, in my hair.
Bubbles in my hair, in my hair.
Bubbles in my hair and I don't even care.
Bubbles in my hair, in my hair.

Bubbles in the air, in the air.
Bubbles in the air, in the air.
Bubbles in the air, pop them if you dare.
Bubbles in the air, in the air.

Bubble Song by Pam Schiller (Tune: K-K-K-Katie)
B-B-B-Bubbles, beautiful bubbles,
Will you float upon the air or will you soar?
B-B-B-Bubbles, beautiful bubbles,
Oh, it's b-b-b-bubbles we adore.

B-B-B-Bubbles, beautiful bubbles,
Blow just a few and you'll want more.
B-B-B-Bubbles, beautiful bubbles,
Oh, it's b-b-b-bubbles we adore.

THE COMPLETE RESOURCE BOOK FOR INFANTS

Bye Baby Bunting (Traditional)

Bye baby bunting

Daddy's gone a-hunting

Mommy's gone a-milking

Sister's gone a-silking

Brother's gone to buy a skin

To wrap the baby bunting in.

Chew, Chew, Chew Your Food by Pam Schiller (Tune: Row, Row, Row Your Boat)

Chew, chew, chew your food

A little at a time

Chew it slow, chew it fast,

Chew it to this rhyme.

Cleanup Time by Pam Schiller (Tune: Do You Know the Muffin Man?)

Oh, can you put the toys away,

Toys away, toys away?

Oh, can you put the toys away?

It's time to end our play.

Close Your Eyes (Tune: London Bridge)

Close your eyes and go to sleep.

Go to sleep, go to sleep.

Close your eyes and go to sleep,

Little (insert child's name).

Drink, Drink, Drink Your Milk by Pam Schiller (Tune: Row, Row, Row Your Boat)

Drink, drink, drink your milk

A little at a time.

Drink it slow, drink it fast,

Drink it to this rhyme.

Dirty Old Bill (Tune: Turkey in the Straw)

I know a man named Dirty Old Bill.

He lives on top of a garbage hill.

Oh, he never took a bath and he never will.

Pheew-eew! Dirty Old Bill!

Evan's Tub Time by Richele Bartkowiak (Tune: Rock-a-Bye Baby)

Splishin' and a splashin'

In the bathtub.

When we take a bath

We clean and we scrub.

With our wash cloth

And a little shampoo.

And when it's all over

We smell good as new.

Splishin' and a splashin'

That's what we do.

Don't forget Ducky

He likes it too.

Watchin' the bubbles

Dance in the tub.

Oh how we love bath time

Rub-a-dub-dub!

Eyes, Ears, Nose, and Mouth by Pam Schiller (Tune: Head, Shoulders, Knees, and Toes)

Eyes, ears, nose, and mouth—nose and mouth,

Eyes, ears, nose, and mouth—nose and mouth,

Two eyes, two ears, one nose, one mouth—

Eyes, ears, nose, and mouth—nose and mouth.

Five Little Speckled Frogs (Traditional)

(Five children sit in a row and the other children sit in a circle around them. All children act out the words to the song.)

Five little speckled frogs (hold up five fingers)

Sitting on a speckled log

Eating some most delicious bugs. (pretend to

eat bugs)

Yum! Yum!

One jumped into the pool, (one child from center

jumps back into the circle)

Where it was nice and cool. (cross arms over chest

and shiver)

Now there are four little speckled frogs

Burr-ump!

Friendship Song by Pam Schiller (Tune: Do You Know the Muffin Man?)

Do you know you are my friend,
You are my friend, you are my friend?
Do you know you are my friend?
I like to play with you.

Hand Washing Song by Pam Schiller (Tune: The Farmer in the Dell)

It's time to wash our hands.
It's time to wash our hands.
Hi, ho, hooray for hands,
It's time to wash our hands.

Let's turn the water on.
Let's turn the water on.
Hi ho, hooray for hands,
It's time to wash our hands.

Now add a little soap.
Now add a little soap.
Hi, ho, hooray for hands,
It's time to wash our hands.

Don't forget your fingers.
Don't forget your fingers.
Hi, ho, hooray for hands,
It's time to wash our hands.

We dry our hands at last.
We dry our hands at last.
Hi, ho, hooray for hands,
We washed and dried our hands.

Head, Shoulders, Knees, and Toes (Traditional)

(Touch body parts as they are mentioned in the song.)

Head, shoulders, knees, and toes,
Knees and toes.
Head and shoulders, knees and toes,
Knees and toes.
Eyes and ears and mouth and nose.
Head, shoulders, knees, and toes,
Knees and toes.

Hello, Maria (Tune: Are You Sleeping?)

Hello, Maria,

Hello, Maria.

How are you?

How are you?

I'm so glad to see you.

I'm so glad to see you.

Let's go play.

Let's go play.

I Am Special by Pam Schiller (Tune: Are You Sleeping?)

I am special, I am special.

Yes, I am. Yes, I am.

Special to my mommy,

Special to my daddy,

Special, special me.

Special, special me.

If You're Happy and You Know It (Traditional)

If you're happy and you know it, clap your hands. (clap hands twice)

If you're happy and you know it, clap your hands. (repeat)

If you're happy and you know it then your face will surely show it. (point to face)

If you're happy and you know it, clap your hands. (clap hands twice)

Additional verses:

…Stomp your feet. (stomp feet twice)

…Shout hurray! (raise hand)

…Point to a circle.

…Point to the color red.

Itsy Bitsy Spider (Traditional)

The itsy bitsy spider

Went up the water spout.

Down came the rain

And washed the spider out.

Up came the sun

And dried up all the rain.

And the itsy bitsy spider

Went up the spout again.

Lavender's Blue (Traditional)
Lavender's blue, dilly, dilly,
Lavender's green.
When you are King, dilly, dilly,
I shall be Queen.

Who told you so, dilly, dilly,
Who told you so?
'Twas my own heart, dilly, dilly,
That told me so.
Call up your friends, dilly, dilly
Set them to work.
Some to the plough, dilly, dilly,
Some to the fork.

Some to the hay, dilly, dilly,
Some to thresh corn.
Whilst you and I, dilly, dilly,
Keep ourselves warm.

Lavender's blue, dilly, dilly,
Lavender's green.
When you are King, dilly, dilly,
I shall be Queen.

Who told you so, dilly, dilly,
Who told you so?
'Twas my own heart, dilly, dilly,
That told me so.

Little Hunk of Tin adapted by Pam Schiller (Tune: I'm a Little Acorn Brown)
I'm a little hunk of tin.
Nobody knows what shape I'm in.
Got four wheels and a tank of gas.
I can go but not too fast.

Chorus:
Honk, honk. (pull ear)
Rattle, rattle. (shake head side to side)
Crash, crash. (push chin)
Beep, beep. (push nose)
(Sing twice)

I'm a little ice cream truck.
I wibble, wobble like a duck.
Got four wheels and lots of cream,
I make children shout and scream.

chorus

I'm a little yellow bus,
Newly painted, not a spot of rust,
Brand-new wheels and kids inside.
Hold on tight for a happy ride.

chorus

Little Ant's Hill (Tune: Dixie)
Oh, I stuck my foot
On a little ant's hill,
And the little ant said,
"You better be still,
Take it off! Take it off!
Take it off! Remove it!"

Oh, I didn't take it off,
And the little ant said,
"If you don't take it off
You'll wish you had.
Take it off! Take it off!"
Ouch! I removed it!

Mary Had a Little Lamb (Traditional)
Mary had a little lamb, little lamb, little lamb.
Mary had a little lamb,
Its fleece was white as snow.

Everywhere that Mary went,
Mary went, Mary went,
Everywhere that Mary went
The lamb was sure to go.

Now It's Time to Say Goodbye by Pam Schiller (Tune: Do You Know the Muffin Man?)

Now it's time to say goodbye,

Say good-bye, say goodbye.

Now it's time to say goodbye.

I'll see you in the morning.

Oh, Dear, What Can the Matter Be? (Traditional—adapted by Pam Schiller)

Oh, dear, what can the matter be?

Oh, dear, what can the matter be?

Oh, dear, what can the matter be?

I think you are calling me.

I'm here to take care of you, dear.

I'm here to take care of you, dear.

I'm here to take care of you, dear.

Let's wipe away that tear.

Oh, Do You Know by Pam Schiller (Tune: Do You Know the Muffin Man?)

Oh, do you know I love you so,

Love you so, love you so?

Oh, do you know I love you so,

I surely hope you know.

Popcorn Pop by Pam Schiller (Tune: Row, Row, Row Your Boat)

Pop, pop, pop, popcorn

Pop it everywhere

Poppity, poppity, poppity, poppity.

Popcorn in the air.

Pop…pop…pop…pop.

Poppity, poppity, poppity, pop!

Pop! Goes the Weasel (Traditional)

(Have the children walk in a circle until they hear the words, "Pop! Goes the weasel."

When they hear these words, they jump.)

All around the mulberry bush,

The monkey chased the weasel.

The monkey thought it was all in fun,

Pop! Goes the weasel.

A penny for a spool of thread,
A penny for a needle,
That's the way the money goes-
Pop! Goes the weasel.

All around the mulberry bush,
The monkey chased the weasel.
The monkey thought it was all in fun,
Pop! Goes the weasel.

Rock-a-Bye Baby (Traditional)
Rock-a-bye, baby,
In the treetop,
When the wind blows
The cradle will rock;
When the bough breaks
The cradle will fall,
And down will come
   baby,
Cradle and all.

Rock-a-bye, baby,
Your cradle is green,
Father's a King
And Mother's a Queen.
Sister's a Lady
And wears a gold ring,
Brother's a drummer
And plays for the king.

Rock-a-bye baby,
Way up on high,
Never mind baby,
Mother is 'nigh.
Up to the ceiling,
Down to the ground,
Rock-a-bye baby,
Up hill and down.

Row, Row, Row Your Boat (Traditional)

Row, row, row your boat
Gently down the stream.
Merrily, merrily, merrily, merrily
Life is but a dream.

Six White Ducks (Traditional)

Six white ducks that I once knew,
Fat ducks, skinny ducks, they were, too.
But the one little duck with the feather on her back,
She ruled the others with a quack, quack, quack!

Down to the river they would go,
Wibble, wobble, wibble, wobble all in a row.
But the one little duck with the feather on her back,
She ruled the others with a quack, quack, quack!

Skidamarink (Traditional)

Skidamarink a dink a dink,
Skidamarink a doo,
I love you.
Skidamarink a dink a dink,
Skidamarink a doo,
I love you.

I love you in the morning
And in the afternoon,
I love you in the evening
And underneath the moon;
Oh, skidamarink a dink a dink,
Skidamarink a doo,
I love you!

Smile Song by Pam Schiller (Tune: Row, Row, Row Your Boat)

Smile, smile, smile at me
And I will smile at you.
Every time you give a smile
It always turns to two.

Tell Me Why (Traditional)

Tell me why the stars do shine,

Tell me why the ivy twines,

Tell me why the skies are blue,

And I will tell you just why I love you.

This Is Quinn by Pam Schiller (Tune: Here We Go 'Round the Mulberry Bush)

(Substitute names and characteristics to children in your classroom.)

This is Quinn over here, over here.

He has on a bright blue shirt.

This is Quinn, our new friend.

We're so glad he's here.

This Is the Way Wash Our Face (Tune: Here We Go 'Round the Mulberry Bush)

This is the way we wash our face,

Scrub our cheeks, scrub our ears.

This is the way we wash our face,

Until we're squeaky clean.

Three White Mice by Barbara Drolshagen and JoAnn Rajchal (Tune: Three Blind Mice)

Three white mice, three white mice.

See how they dance, see how they dance.

They danced and danced for the farmer's wife.

She played for them on a silver fife.

Did you ever see such a sight in your life,

As three white mice?

Too-Ra-Loo-Ra-Loo-Ral (Traditional)

Too-ra-loo-ra-loo-ral,

Too-ra-loo-ra-li,

Too-ra-loo-ra-loo-ral,

Hush, now don't you cry!

Too-ra-loo-ra-loo-ral,

Too-ra-loo-ra-li,

Too-ra-loo-ra-loo-ral,

That's an Irish lullaby.

Tooth Brushing Song (Tune: Here We Go 'Round the Mulberry Bush)

This is the way we brush our teeth

Brush our teeth, brush our teeth.

This is the way we brush our teeth

Every day and night.

We move the brush up and down,

Up and down, up and down.

We move the brush up and down

Every time we brush.

Twinkle, Twinkle, Little Star (Traditional)

Twinkle, twinkle, little star,

How I wonder what you are!

Up above the world so high,

Like a diamond in the sky.

Twinkle, twinkle, little star,

How I wonder what you are!

Wheels on the Bus (Traditional)

The wheels on the bus go round and round. (move hands in circular motion)

Round and round, round and round.

The wheels on the bus go round and round,

All around the town.   (extend arms up and out)

Additional verses:

The windshield wipers go swish, swish, swish. (sway hands back and forth)

The baby on the bus goes, "Wah, wah, wah."

(rub eyes)

People on the bus go up and down. (stand up, sit down)

The horn on the bus goes beep, beep, beep.

(pretend to beep horn)

The money on the bus goes clink, clink, clink. (drop change in)

The driver on the bus says, "Move on back." (point thumb over shoulder)

Where Is Thumbkin? (Traditional)

Where is Thumbkin? (hands behind back)

Where is Thumbkin?

Here I am. Here I am. (bring out right thumb, then left)

How are you today, sir? (bend right thumb)

Very well, I thank you. (bend left thumb)

Run away. Run away. (put right thumb behind back, then left thumb behind back)

Other verses:

Where is Pointer?

Where is Middle One?

Where is Ring Finger?

Where is Pinky?

Where are all of them?

Fingerplays

All By Myself
These are things I can do
All by myself. (point to self)
I can comb my hair and fasten my shoe (point to hair and shoe)
All by myself. (point to self)
I can wash my hands and wash my face (pretend to wash)
All by myself. (point to self)
I can put my toys and blocks in place (pretend to put things away)
All by myself. (point to self)

Clap Your Hands
(Suit actions to the words.)
Clap your hands 1-2-3.
Clap your hands just like me.
Wiggle your fingers 1-2-3.
Wiggle your fingers just like me.

Eye Winker
Eye winker, (point to eye)
Tom Tinker, (touch ears)
Nose smeller, (touch nose)
Mouth eater, (touch mouth)
Chin chopper, (tap chin)
Chin chopper, (tap chin again)
Chin chopper chin. (tap chin three times)

Fabulous Fingers by Pam Schiller
My fingers are so fabulous. (hold hands up)
Just look what they can do.
They can wiggle, they can dance, (wiggle fingers)
And take a bow or two. (fold fingers at knuckle)
They can wave, they can point, (wave)
And even blow a kiss. (blow on hand)
But what they like most— (hold a friend's hand)
Is to hold a hand like this.

Falling Leaves by Pam Schiller

Little leaves are falling down, (wiggle finger downward)

Red and yellow, orange and brown. (count on fingers)

Whirling, twirling 'round and 'round,(twirl fingers)

Falling softly to the ground. (wiggle finger downward to the ground)

Five Little Fingers

One little finger standing on its own. (hold up index finger)

Two little fingers, now they're not alone. (hold up middle finger)

Three little fingers happy as can be. (hold up ring finger)

Four little fingers go walking down the street. (hold up all fingers)

Five little fingers. This one is a thumb. (hold up four fingers and thumb)

Wave bye-bye 'cause now we are done. (wave bye-bye)

I Have a Little Wagon

I have a little wagon, (hold hand out palm up)

It goes everywhere with me. (move hand around)

I can pull it. (pull hand toward you)

I can push it. (push hand away from you)

I can turn it upside down. (turn hand upside down)

Jack-in-the-Box

Jack-in-the-box (tuck thumb into fist)

Oh, so still.

Won't you come out? (raise hand slightly)

Yes, I will. (pop thumb out of fist)

Little Red Apple

A little red apple grew high in a tree. (point up)

I looked up at it. (shade eyes and look up)

It looked down at me. (shade eyes and look down)

"Come down, please," I said. (use hand to motion downward)

And that little red apple fell right on my head. (tap the top of your head)

Open, Shut Them

Open, shut them.

Open, shut them.

Give a little clap.

Open, shut them.

Open, shut them.

Put them in your lap.

Walk them, walk them, (walk fingers up chest to chin)

Walk them, walk them.

Way up to your chin.

Walk them, walk them, (walk fingers around face, but not into mouth)

Walk them, walk them,

But don't let them walk in.

Slowly, Slowly

Slowly, slowly, very slowly (walk finger up
   arm slowly)

Creeps the garden snail.

Slowly, slowly, very slowly

Up the wooden rail.

Quickly, quickly, very quickly (run fingers
   up arm)

Runs the little mouse.

Quickly, quickly, very quickly

Round about the house.

Ten Little Fingers

I have ten little fingers, (hold up ten fingers)

And they all belong to me. (point to self)

I can make them do things. (wiggle fingers)

Do you want to see? (tilt head)

I can make them point. (point)

I can make them hold. (hold fingertips together)

I can make them dance (dance fingers on arm)

And then I make them fold. (fold hands in lap)

Thelma Thumb

(Move thumb as directed.)

Thelma Thumb is up and Thelma Thumb is down.

Thelma Thumb is dancing all around the town.

Dance her on your shoulders, dance her on your head.

Dance her on your knees and tuck her into bed.

Name other fingers: Phillip Pointer, Terry Tall, Richie Ring, Baby Finger, and Finger Family, and dance them on other body parts.

There Once Was a Turtle

There was a little turtle (make a fist)

He lived in a box. (draw a square in the air)

He swam in a puddle. (pretend to swim)

He climbed on the rocks. (pretend to climb)

He snapped at a mosquito. (use your hand to make a snapping motion)

He snapped at a flea. (snapping motion)

He snapped at a minnow. (snapping motion)

And he snapped at me. (snapping motion)

He caught the mosquito. (clap hands)

He caught the flea. (clap hands)

He caught the minnow. (clap hands)

But he didn't catch me. (wave index finger as if saying no-no)

This Little Finger

This little finger holds on tight. (wiggle each finger as it is mentioned)

This little finger points just right.

This little finger helps wave bye.

This little finger wipes my eye.

This little finger holds, points, waves, and wipes.

Sweet little hands hold on tight.

Two Little Blackbirds

Two little blackbirds (hold up index finger of
   each hand)
Sitting on a hill.
One named Jack. (hold right hand/finger
   forward)
One named Jill. (hold left
   hand/finger forward)
Fly away, Jack. (wiggle right finger and
place behind your back)
Fly away, Jill. (wiggle left finger and place behind your back)
Come back, Jack. (bring right hand back)
Come back, Jill. (bring left hand back)

Two Little Houses

Two little houses,
Closed up tight. (close fists)
Let's open the windows,
And let in some light. (open fists)
And let in the light.

Rhymes and Chants

After My Bath

After my bath I try, try, try

To rub with a towel 'til I'm dry, dry, dry.

Hands to dry, and fingers and toes,

And two wet legs and a shiny nose.

Just think how much less time it'd take

If I were a dog and could shake, shake, shake!

Baby Feet by Pam Schiller

I love your baby feet. (hold baby's feet up so he can see them)

I love your little toes. (touch baby's toes)

Your little feet are sweet. (touch baby's feet to your cheek)

Let's touch them to your nose. (touch baby's feet to his nose)

Walk, walk, walk little feet. (move feet as if walking)

Run, run, run little feet. (move baby's feet faster)

Dance, dance, dance little feet. (move baby's feet in circular motion)

Sweet, sweet, sweet little feet. (touch baby's feet to your cheek)

Be Very Quiet

Shhh—be very quiet,

Shhh—be very still.

Fold your busy little hands,

Close your sleepy little eyes.

Shhh—be very quiet.

Bella, Bella

Bella, bella, bella. (say slowly while gently stroking baby's cheek)

(hesitate)

Bruta, bruta, bruta. (say rapidly while gently tapping baby's cheek)

THE COMPLETE RESOURCE BOOK FOR INFANTS

Bounce Baby

Bounce baby, bounce.

Bounce baby, bounce.

Bounce up.

Bounce back.

Bounce baby, bounce.

Bounce baby, bounce.

Bounce right into my arms.

Bouncing Ball

I'm bouncing, bouncing, bouncing everywhere

I bounce and bounce into the air.

I'm bouncing, bouncing like a ball.

I bounce and bounce until I fall. (children drop to the floor)

Caterpillar

"Who's that ticklin' my back?" said the wall. (crawl fingers up baby's arm)

"Me," said a small caterpillar, "I'm learning to crawl."

Clickety Clack

*(Make a train by lining children up and asking them to hold on to each other's waists.
Move through the room saying the chant.)*

Clickety, clickety, clack.

Clickety, clickety, clack.

Clickety, clickety, clickety, clickety,

Clickety, clickety clack.

Dry Diaper Chant

I'm changing your diaper, Sweetie Pie.

In just a minute you'll be dry, dry, dry.

Family Music

(Use the names of the children in the class)

Mother plays the violin, (pretend to play instruments)

Father plays the flute.

Little Richele plays the horn,

Toot, toot, toot, toot, toot!

Fee-Fi-Fo-Fum

Fee-Fi-Fo-Fum,

Fee-Fi-Fo-Fum,

Fee-Fi-Fo-Fum,

Rum Tum Tum!

Five Fingers on Each Hand

(Suit actions to the words.)

I have five fingers on each hand,

Ten toes on my two feet.

Two ears, two eyes,

One nose, one mouth,

With which to sweetly speak.

My hands can clap, my feet can tap,

My eyes can clearly see.

My ears can hear,

My nose can sniff,

My mouth can say I'm me.

Gelatin Jigglers #1 by Pam Schiller

Gelatin Jigglers in my tummy.

Gelatin Jigglers yummy, yummy, yummy.

Gelatin Jigglers wiggle, jiggle, wiggle.

Galatin Jigglers make me giggle.

Gelatin Jigglers #2 by Pam Schiller

Gelatin Jigglers on my tray.

They make me laugh and want to play.

Wiggle, giggle, smooth and cool.

What a treat to eat at school.

Grasping Rhyme by Pam Schiller

I place my finger in your left palm,

You grab it and hold on tight.

Your left hand is growing stronger,

Now let's try it with your right.

Hello, Friends

Hello, good friend.
Hello, good friend.
How are you, Kathy?

Hey, Diddle Diddle

Hey, diddle diddle, the cat and the fiddle.
The cow jumped over the moon.
The little dog laughed to see such a sight,
And the dish ran away with the spoon.

Hickory, Dickory, Dock

Hickory, dickory, dock,
The mouse ran up the clock.
The clock struck one,
The mouse ran down.
Hickory dickory dock.

Humpty Dumpty

Humpty Dumpty sat on a wall.
Humpty Dumpty had a great fall.
All the King's horses and all the King's men
Couldn't put Humpty Dumpty together again.

I Can by Pam Schiller

I can wave my hand—wave, wave, wave. (wave)
I can shake my head—shake, shake, shake.
   (shake head yes and no)
I can move around—move, move, move. (crawl or
   walk depending on ability)
I can smile—ha, ha, ha. (smile)
And I can blow you a kiss—smooch, smooch,
   smooch. (blow a kiss)

I Can, Can You? by Pam Schiller
(Suit actions to words.)
I can put my hands up high. Can you?
I can wink my eye. Can you?
I can stick out my tongue. Can you?
I can nod my head. Can you?
I can kiss my toe. Can you?
I can pull on my ear. Can you?
I can wrinkle my nose. Can you?
I can give myself a great big hug. Can you?
And if I give my hug to you, will you give yours to me?

Ice Cream Chant
You scream.
I scream.
We all scream for ice cream.

I See the Moon
I see the moon
And the moon sees me.
Here's to the moon
And here's to me.

Little Hands by Pam Schiller
Little hands, sweet hands,
Hands to do so much.
Hands to hold,
Hands to touch,
Little hands, sweet hands,
Hands to do so much.

Morning Greeting by Pam Schiller
(Substitute babies' names.)
Madison, Madison,
Howdy-do.
Hello. Good-day.
How are you?

Motor Boat

Motor boat, motor boat, go so slow. (walk in a circle slowly while chanting)

Motor boat, motor boat, go so fast. (walk quickly while continuing to chant)

My Body Talks by Pam Schiller

When I want to say, "Hello," I wave my hand.

When I want to say, "No," I shake my head from side to side.

When I want to say, "Yes," I nod my head up and down.

When I want to say, "Good job," I stick up my thumb.

When I want to say, "I disagree," I turn my thumb down.

When I want to celebrate a success, I clap my hands.

When I want to say, "Enough," or "Stop," I hold my hand out.

When I want to say, "Come here," I wave my hand toward me.

When I want to say, "Goodbye," I wave my hand or blow you a kiss.

When I want to say, "I love you," I wrap my arms around you and squeeze.

My Family by Pam Schiller

Mommy and I dance and sing.

Daddy and I laugh and play.

Mommy, Daddy, and I

Dance and sing,

Laugh and play,

Kiss and hug,

A zillion times a day.

Old Gray Cat

The old gray cat is sleeping, sleeping, sleeping.

The old gray cat is sleeping in the house. (one child, the cat, curls up, pretending
   to sleep)

The little mice are creeping, creeping, creeping.

The little mice are creeping through the house. (other children, the mice, creep around
   the cat)

The old gray cat is waking, waking, waking.

The old gray cat is waking in the house. (cat slowly sits up and stretches)

The old gray cat is chasing, chasing, chasing.

The old gray cat is chasing through the house. (cat chases mice)

All the mice are squealing, squealing, squealing.

All the mice are squealing through the house. (mice squeal; when cat catches a mouse,

that mouse becomes the cat)

Pat-a-Cake

Pat-a-cake, pat-a-cake, baker's man. (clap hands together)

Bake me a cake as fast as you can.

Roll it (roll hands over each other)

And pat it (pat hands together)

And mark it with "B" (draw B in the air or on baby's tummy)

And put it in the oven for Baby and me. (tickle baby's tummy)

A Ram Sam Sam

A ram sam sam (hit one fist on top of the other)

A ram sam sam (hit opposite fist on top of the other)

Goolie goolie goolie, goolie (roll hands arm over arm)

A ram sam sam (hit fists again)

A raffy a raffy (lift arms)

Goolie goolie goolie (roll hands again)

And a RAM SAM SAM! (hit fists again)

Ride a Little Horsie

Ride a little horsie,

Go to town.

Be very careful,

So you don't fall down.

Rock and Go Crawling Chant

Rock, rock, rock,

Go, go, go.

Rock, rock, rock,

To and fro.

Go, go, go

Just like so.

Rock, rock,

Go, go!

Rocking To and Fro

Rocking, rocking,

Rocking to and fro.

Rocking, rocking,

Back and forth we go.

'Round the House

'Round the house, (use index finger to trace a circle on the child's open palm)

'Round the house,

Goes the little mousie.

Up the stairs, (walk index finger and middle finger up the child's arm)

Up the stairs,

In his little housie. (tickle the child under her arm or under her chin.)

Rub-a-Dub-Dub Babies by Pam Schiller

Rub-a-dub-dub, (gently rock box or basket)

Three babes in a tub,

And who do you think they be?

Gabrielle, Madison, and Austin (insert names of babies)

Turn them around all three. (turn the box or basket)

Seesaw, Millie McGraw

Seesaw, Millie McGraw,

Rocking slow,

Back and forth we go,

See-saw, Millie McGraw.

Shake Your Pudding by Pam Schiller

Shake, shake, shake your pudding.

Shake it here, shake it there.

Shake it everywhere.

Shake it twice.

Shake it nice.

Shake it here, shake it there.

Shake it everywhere.

Star Light, Star Bright

Star light, star bright,
First star I've seen tonight.
I wish I may, I wish I might,
Have this wish I wish tonight.

Stretching Chant

(Suit actions to the words.)
Stretch to the windows,
Stretch to the door,
Stretch up to the ceiling,
And bend to the floor.

Stretching Fun

I stretch and stretch and find it fun (stretch)
To try to reach up to the sun. (reach hands up)
I bend and bend to touch the ground, (touch the ground)
Then I twist and twist around. (twist side to side)

Teddy Bear, Teddy Bear

(Suit actions to words.)
Teddy bear, teddy bear,
Turn around.
Teddy bear, teddy bear,
Touch the ground.
Teddy bear, teddy bear,
Touch your shoe.
Teddy bear, teddy bear,
Say how-di-do.
Teddy bear, teddy bear,
Go up the stairs.
Teddy bear, teddy bear,
Say your prayers.
Teddy bear, teddy bear,
Turn out the light.
Teddy bear, teddy bear,
Say goodnight.

Thank You

(Suit actions to words.)

My hands say thank you

With a clap, clap, clap.

My feet say thank you

With a tap, tap, tap.

Clap, clap, clap.

Tap, tap, tap.

I turn around

Touch the ground

And with a bow,

I say…thank you, now.

This Little Piggy

This little piggy went to market, (wiggle big toe)

This little piggy stayed home, (wiggle second toe)

This little piggy had roast beef, (wiggle middle toe)

This little piggy had none, (wiggle fourth toe)

And this little piggy cried,

"Wee-wee-wee!" all the way home. (wiggle little toe)

Tiny Seeds

Tiny seed planted just right, (children tuck themselves into a ball)

Not a breath of air, not a ray of light.

Rain falls slowly to and fro,

And now the seed begins to grow. (children begin to unfold)

Slowly reaching for the light,

With all its energy, all its might.

The little seed's work is almost done,

To grow up tall and face the sun. (children stand up tall with arms stretched out)

Toes to Ears

Toes to toes, that's how it goes!
Toes to ears, those ears are dears!

Toes to Nose

Toes to toes, that's how it goes.
Toes to nose, those silly toes!

Wake Up, Jack-in-the-Box

(Suit actions to the words.)
Jack-in-the-box, jack-in-the-box,
Wake up, wake up, somebody knocks.
One time, two times, three times, four.
Jack pops out of his little round door.

Washington Square

From here to there (begin tracing a square)
To Washington Square.
When I get near
I'll kiss your hair. (gently kiss the child's
hair)

We Can

(Suit actions to words.)
We can jump, jump, jump,
We can hop, hop, hop,
We can clap, clap, clap,
We can stop, stop, stop.

We can nod our heads for yes,
We can shake our heads for no.
We can bend our knees a tiny bit
And sit down slow.

We're Here for Each Other by Pam Schiller

Every day I'm here for you.
I give you a smile for every coo.
I get your bottle and keep you dry.
I hold you close when you cry.

Every day you're here for me.
When I'm blue you seem to see.
You smile and coo as if to say,
I'm here to cheer you through the day.

Your Fingers Grow Stronger by Pam Schiller

Your fingers grow stronger every day
I feel them when we hold hands
I feel them when we play.
Think of all the things you can do:
Hold a rattle, point to a friend,
And soon—pick up a pea, tie a shoe.

Tongue Twister Fun

Recite tongue twisters to little ones. They are very receptive to sounds. Of course, they may not know what you are saying, but the repetitive sounds will help develop their receptive language skills. Plus, they are just plain fun to do! Say each line three times quickly.

- She sells seashells by the seashore.
- Three tricky tigers.
- Peter piper picked a peck of pickled peppers.
- How much wood would a woodchuck chuck if a woodchuck could chuck wood?

Stories

Mr. Wiggle and Mr. Waggle (participation story)

This is Mr. Wiggle *(Hold up right hand, make a fist but keep the thumb pointing up. Wiggle thumb.)* and this is Mr. Waggle. *(Hold up left hand, make a fist but keep the thumb pointing up. Wiggle thumb.)* Mr. Wiggle and Mr. Waggle live in houses on top of different hills and there is a hill between their homes.

When Mr. Wiggle goes to visit Mr. Waggle he has to go down the hill and up the hill and down the hill and up the hill to get to Mr. Waggle's house. *(Move right hand up and down in a wave fashion to go with text.)*

When Mr. Waggle goes to visit Mr. Wiggle he has to do the same thing. He goes down the hill and up the hill and down the hill and up the hill to get to Mr. Wiggle's house. *(Use wave motion to follow text.)*

One day Mr. Wiggle and Mr. Waggle decided to go visit each other at the same time. They opened their doors and came outside at the same time. *(Take thumbs from inside the fist.)* They went down the hill, up the hill *(Use wave motion to follow text.)*, and they met right on top of the hill between their homes.

They talked and laughed and visited *(Wiggle thumbs.)* until the sun went down. Then they went down the hill and up the hill, and down the hill and up the hill, to their own homes. *(Make a wave motion with both hands to follow the text.)* They opened their doors *(Open fists.)*, pop, went inside *(Tuck thumbs inside fists.)*, pop, closed their doors *(Close fists.)*, pop, and went to sleep. *(Place your head on your hands.)*

Games and Dances

Amazing Mazes

Create a maze with boxes, chairs, sheets, and pillows. Encourage children to navigate the maze.

Back Thing

Play Back Thing with the children. Hold an empty paper towel tube against your chest. Get the children to chase you around the room. Suddenly change the game by turning around and holding the empty paper towel tube out toward the children and saying "Back Thing." This is the signal for the children to turn and run from you. When you catch them start the game over. Hide the tube against your chest and run from the children.

Bumblebee Buzz

"Fly" your pointer finger through the air like a bumblebee around a baby. Make a buzzing sound as you move. After a few seconds, use your pointer finger to tickle the baby under the chin, under the arm, or lightly on the stomach.

Cat and Mouse

This is a simple game of chase where you or one child pretends to be the Cat and the rest of the children pretend to be Mice. The Cat chases the Mice. The Mouse who is tagged becomes the next Cat. You might also use the rhyme, "Old Gray Cat," (see page 209 to play a version of this game.

London Bridge Is Falling Down

Have two children face each other, hold hands, and then raise their arms to make a bridge. Have the rest of the children circle under the bridge singing the song, "London Bridge Is Falling Down." On the line "My fair lady," the children making the bridge lower their arms and encircle the child who is between them. During the second verse of the song, the "bridge children" gently rock the child caught in the bridge back and forth. At the end of the second verse, the child is released and the game begins again.

London Bridge is falling down,
Falling down, falling down.
London Bridge is falling down,
My fair lady.

Take the key and lock her up,
Lock her up, lock her up.
Take the key and lock her up,
My fair lady.

(repeat first verse)

Musical Freeze

Invite your walkers to dance or move in a circle while a favorite song plays. When you stop the music, they stop moving. When you start the music again, they start moving.

Musical Hide and Seek

Hide a musical toy just out of sight and see if children can find it.

Partner Ball Play

Have two children sit facing each other and spread their legs. Show them how to roll a ball back and forth to each other.

Ring Around the Rosy

Children hold hands and walk in a circle singing the song. When they come to the line "all fall down," they all fall down.

Ring around the rosy,
A pocket full of posies,
Ashes, ashes,
All fall down.

Whoops, Johnny!

Hold an infant's hand and touch each finger, beginning with the pinky, as you say "Johnny." Slide your finger between the infant's forefinger and thumb and back again as you say "Whoops, Johnny." Touch baby's fingers again on the remaining "Johnny's."

Johnny, Johnny,
Johnny, Johnny,
Whoops, Johnny.
Whoops, Johnny.
Johnny, Johnny,
Johnny.

Recipes

Safety Note: As much as possible, allow children to participate in cooking activities. Before allowing children to help with food preparation and serving, always check for allergies. Make sure, if heat is used, you provide plenty of supervision.

No-Cook Food Recipes

Baggie Ice Cream

One serving:

½ cup milk

1 tablespoon sugar

¼ teaspoon vanilla

small resealable plastic bag

large resealable plastic bag

3 tablespoons rock salt

Place the milk, sugar, and vanilla in the small bag and seal it. Place the small bag, the rock salt, and ice cubes in the large bag and seal. Shake.

Gelatin Jigglers

Mix flavored gelatin with half the amount of water suggested on the box. Add thinly sliced bananas or small pieces of diced apples. Let congeal. Let children use shape cookie cutters to help cut the gelatin.

Individual Puddings

Put one tablespoon of instant pudding mix in a small jar and add warm milk. Screw the lid on securely and let the children shake the jar. In a few minutes the pudding will set.

Trail Mix

Mix wheat cereal, rice cereal, raisins, and miniature marshmallows to make a great finger food snack. Older infants love to create the mix and their small hands pick up just the right amount of each ingredient.

Art and Craft Recipes

Note: When possible, allow children to help you mix art mediums. However, make sure you check for allergies prior to participation, and always keep children away from any heat sources.

Bubble Soap
1 teaspoon glycerin
½ cup liquid detergent
½ cup water

Mix all ingredients and stir gently. For best results, let the mixture sit overnight before blowing bubbles.

Colored Glue
Add tempera paint to glue to make various colors. Let children squeeze "paint" their pictures instead of painting with brushes.

Colored Rock Salt
Dye rock salt by placing food coloring in rubbing alcohol and letting the salt sit in the mixture for about 10 minutes. Drain on a paper towel.

Face Paint
2 tablespoons cold cream
½ teaspoon glycerin
1 teaspoon cornstarch
1 teaspoon powdered tempera paint

Stir ingredients together until well mixed.

Fingerpaint #1
Pour a tablespoon of liquid starch onto paper or directly onto a tabletop. Sprinkle on a little powdered tempera paint. Let the children mix with their fingers. To add texture to the paint, add a tablespoon of sand.

Fingerpaint Recipe #2

⅓ cup of cornstarch

¾ cup of cold water

1 envelope Knox gelatin

¼ cup of cold water

2 cups hot water

½ cup of Ivory Flakes (or Ivory Snow)

Dissolve ⅓ cup of cornstarch in ¾ cup of cold water. Dissolve 1 envelope of Knox gelatin in ¼ cup of cold water. Add 2 cups of hot water to the cornstarch mixture and cook. Stir until the mixture is clear. Add the gelatin mixture and stir to blend. Add Ivory Flakes or Ivory Snow. Divide the mixture into containers. Add the desired color of powdered tempera paint to each container.

Fingerpaint Recipe #3

1 cup of laundry starch

½ cup cold water

1 quart boiling water

1 ½ cups soap flakes

½ cup talcum

powdered tempera paint

Mix starch and cold water into a creamy paste. Add boiling water and cook until the mixture becomes transparent or glossy looking. Stir continually. Add talcum and allow the mixture to cool. Add soap flakes and stir until they are evenly distributed. Pour into containers and add powdered tempera paint to color.

Gak

2 cups glue

1 ½ cups tap water

2 teaspoon Borax

1 cup hot water

food coloring

Combine glue, tap water, and food coloring in a bowl. In a larger bowl, dissolve Borax in hot water. Slowly add glue mixture to Borax. It will thicken quickly and be difficult to mix. Mix well and drain off excess water. Let stand for a few minutes. Pour into a shallow tray. Let dry for 10 minutes. Store in a resealable plastic bag or covered container (will keep for 2–3 weeks).

Goop

2 cups salt

1 cup water

1 cup cornstarch

Heat salt and ½ cup water for 4-5 minutes over medium heat. Remove from heat. Add cornstarch and ½ cup water. Return to heat. Stir until mixture thickens. Store in a resealable plastic bag or covered container.

Paste (that will keep)

2 tablespoons flour

2 cups water

½ teaspoon alum

oil of wintergreen (optional)

Mix flour with a small amount of water to form a paste. Pour 2 cups of boiling water into the paste mixture. Boil for 3 minutes in a double boiler. Add alum. Add oil of wintergreen and food coloring if desired.

Playdough

3 cups flour

1 ½ cups salt

3 tablespoons oil

2 tablespoons cream of tartar

3 cups water

Combine all ingredients. Cook the mixture in a saucepan over very low heat until it is no longer sticky to the touch.

Salt Paint

Mix 1 teaspoon salt into fingerpaint and let children enjoy a tactile fingerpainting experience.

Scratch-and-Sniff Paint

Mix flavored gelatin as directed but use only half the amount of water called for. Use the mixture as paint. When it dries children can scratch and sniff it.

Soap Paint

1 cup Ivory Snow

water

Mix in small amounts of water to Ivory Snow until it is the consistency of whipping cream. Beat with an electric mixer until the mixture looks like shaving cream. Add food coloring if desired. Use like finger paint.

Scented Playdough

Add 1 teaspoon of scented extract (peppermint, lemon, and so on) to a basic playdough recipe. Use massage oils in place of extract, if desired.

Soapsuds Clay

¾ cup powdered soap

1 tablespoon warm water

Mix powdered soap and water in a bowl. Beat with an electric mixer until the mixture is the consistency of clay.

Tactile Playdough

Substitute ½ cup of sand for ½ cup of salt in a regular playdough recipe. See page 222 for a playdough recipe.

Textured Paints

Add the following ingredients to one pint of tempera paint to change the consistency.

Slimy paint	add 2 tablespoons corn syrup, such as Karo®
Gritty paint	add ½ teaspoon sand
Slippery paint	add 1 teaspoon glycerin
Lumpy paint	add 1 tablespoon flour
Rough paint	add 1 tablespoon sawdust
Shiny paint	add ½ cup sugar
Sparkly paint	add ½ cup salt (use immediately)
Creamy paint	add ¼ cup liquid starch
Thick paint	mix 3 parts powder to 1 part water

Helpful Hints:

Add liquid soap to all paints to make it easier to wash out of clothes.

Add 1 teaspoon of rubbing alcohol to paint to keep it from souring.

Things to Make

Aroma Bags

Place some potpourri on a 10" square of
mesh. Gather up the mesh to create
a bag and use ribbon or a rubber
band to secure it. **Safety Note**: Check
for allergies before allowing children to
come in contact with Aroma Bags.

Aroma Canisters

Soak cotton balls in scented oil. Put the cotton balls inside a margarine tub with
holes poked in the lid. Make sure lids are taped and/or glued on securely. Scented oils are
available at most candle and craft stores. Chamomile, orange, and lavender are soothing
scents. For your own reference, write the name of the scent on each canister.

Aroma Puffs

Collect six powder puffs. Dab pairs of puffs with extracts such as peppermint, orange,
and vanilla, or use massage oils with interesting aromas. Challenge children to pair the
puffs by matching those that smell alike. For younger children, let them explore the
smells and perhaps select a favorite.

Baby Bells

Sew a jingle bell to a piece of elastic or a child-size scrunchie that will fit loosely around
babies' wrists and ankles. Make sure the bell is sewn on securely. **Safety Note**: Supervise
closely to make sure the bells do not come loose.

Ball Chute

Cut holes in a small cardboard box so that you can fit a paper towel tube through it
diagonally.

Ball Scoop

Cut the bottom and half the sides (up to
the handle) out of an empty, clean,
plastic bleach or similar type bottle to
make a scoop. Teach children how to
catch balls in the scoop.

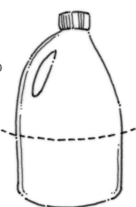

Bird Feeders

Spread a thin layer of peanut butter on a pinecone and then roll it in birdseed. Or, cut a hole in the sides of a milk carton (paper or plastic), stopping about 1" from the bottom, and pour birdseed inside. You might also cut holes to slide a thin dowel rod through to give birds a place to stand. Hang bird feeders outside with yarn, string, or wire.

Bottle Rollers

Fill clean empty plastic half-liter soda bottles with water and add a few drops of food coloring. Place interesting items in the bottles, such as beads, buttons, or confetti. Glue and/or tape the lid on securely.

Bowling Pins

Collect several potato chip cans. Paint them or cover them with colorful contact paper or construction paper. If you would like to weight them, drop a few small stones in each one. Make sure the lids are glued and/or taped on securely.

Box Guitars

Stretch rubber bands around empty shoeboxes. Use rubber bands of different widths and lengths for a variety of tones and pitches.

Box Tunnel

Gather three or four cardboard boxes of graduated sizes that are large enough for children to crawl through. Cut the sides out of the boxes and place them together (smallest to largest) to form a tunnel.

Can Telephones

Make a small hole in the bottom of two empty orange juice cans. Cover any rough edges on the open end of the can with duck tape. Thread a 3' piece of string up through the bottom of one can and tie the end inside the can. Thread the other end of the string into the other can and tie off that end.

hole

tie off the ends of the string

tape edges

Canister Bell

Place a jingle bell inside an empty film canister. Make sure you tape and/or glue the lid on securely.

Canister Shakers

Put paper clips, buttons, or other small objects inside potato chip cans or film canisters. Tape or glue lids on. When you make these with film canisters, even a very small baby can hold them and shake them himself. **Safety Note**: Make sure lids are taped or glued on securely.

Classroom Photo Album

Buy an inexpensive photo album and fill it with photos of the children and teachers in your class. Use photos you take in the classroom and others that families are willing to give you.

Class Photo Baggie Book

Make photocopies of photos of the children that you collected from families. Cut them out and glue them onto 4" x 5" pieces of construction paper. Place photos in resealable plastic bags, putting two photos back to back in each bag. Staple all the bags together at their closed ends (so you can open them). Use colored tape to cover staples.

Color Hoops

Place colored cellophane or plastic wrap in embroidery hoops. If embroidery hoops aren't available, glue the cellophane to heavy cardboard circles you've cut out.

Colored Glasses

Cut eyeglass shapes from poster board and glue colored cellophane in for the lenses, or remove the lenses from old pairs of glasses and replace with cellophane.

Colored Sand

Pour ½ cup of pre-washed sand on a paper plate. Rub colored chalk in the sand until it is the desired color.

Colorscopes

Cover one end of a toilet paper tube with colored cellophane or plastic wrap. Secure with glue and a rubber band or wide tape.

Coaster Bank

Cut a 4" x ½" slot in the top of a plastic lid of a five pound coffee can. Provide plastic coasters to drop through the slot.

Design Bags

Pour ½ cup of liquid starch and 2 tablespoons of tempera paint in large resealable plastic bags. Glue them closed.

Drums

There are several easy ways to make a drum. One is to turn any empty container upside down and beat on the bottom. Coffee cans with plastic lids make good drums, as do oatmeal boxes. You might also stretch canvas or heavy-duty plastic over the open end of a box or other container. Stretch it tight to get the best sound and tape it securely.

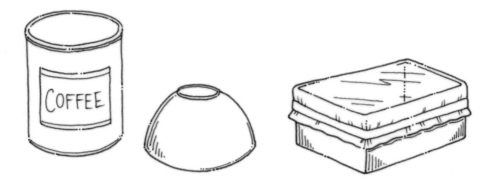

Drumsticks

To make drumsticks, wrap one end of a dowel rod with masking tape or duct tape, place a large eraser on the end of a dowel rod, or use short paintbrushes and pastry brushes.

Face Puzzles

Draw large faces on poster board or cut faces out of magazines and glue them onto poster board. Cut each face into a two- or three-piece puzzle. You can also use enlarged photocopies of children's photographs to make Face Puzzles.

Family Puzzles

Make photocopies of family pictures. Laminate the copies and cut them into puzzle pieces.

Family Roll-Overs

Glue family pictures to empty salt or oatmeal boxes. There are two ways to make this canister. The quickest way is to cover an empty oatmeal box with solid paper and glue interesting photos on the box.

Don't clutter the box—three or four pictures are sufficient. You can use a bigger canister like an ice cream container if you want to. The second and more durable way to make this canister is to cover it with solid contact paper and then glue photograph holders to the container. This allows you to change the photos from time to time and to reuse the canister many times. A small bell inside the box adds a nice extra touch.

Feelings Blocks

Use a marker to draw happy, sad, mad, and surprised faces (you may want to use jack-o-lantern faces) on the fronts and backs of small lunch sacks. Fill the sacks ¾ full with crumpled newspaper. Fold tops down to square off blocks and tape them closed.

Feely Boxes

Line two or three empty boxes with fabrics that have a distinct texture. Cut a 3" size hole in the lids of the boxes and tape the lids onto the boxes.

Feely Cylinders

Cover old-fashioned curlers with tactile fabric like burlap, velvet, fur, satin, art foam, and felt. Use a hot glue gun for best results. Encourage children to match cylinders that feel the same.

Felt Books

Stack five felt squares and sew them together along the left side. Cut felt scraps into geometric shapes and invite the children to use them to create objects, make sets, or reproduce patterns on the sewn felt pages.

Finger Pal Puppets

Draw faces on the fingers of a glove, or glue on pictures of children in your room. Cut the fingers off the glove to make finger puppets.

Friend Puppets

Ask families for photos of their child. Make enlarged copies of the photos. Laminate if desired. Glue the photos onto tongue depressors to make Friend Puppets.

Friendship Match Game

Ask families for photos of their children. Make two photocopies of each baby's picture to make two sets of classroom photos. Glue one set in a colored folder, then laminate or cover with clear contact paper. Leave the other set loose.

Frog Gobbler

Use a paint pen to make large eyes on a meatball press to create a Frog Gobbler. To make it even more realistic you may want to spray paint the press green before painting the eyes.

Funny Hats

Obtain small baseball hats. Glue eyes and a mouth on each hat. Make eyes by cutting a 2' Styrofoam ball in half and then gluing a ½ wiggle eye to each half. Glue a set of eyes on each hat. Cut a piece of red felt to line the underside of the bill. **Safety Note**: Supervise closely to make certain that no small parts come loose.

Garages

Collect several half-pint milk cartons. Wash them out and staple or tape the lids shut. Cut a garage opening in one side of each carton. Cover the cartons with contact paper or construction paper.

Gel Bags

Place ½ cup of hair gel in a resealable plastic bag. Glue it shut.

Hide-and-Seek Bottles

Collect plastic tubes like the ones that socks or tennis balls come in. Cut a piece of construction paper to fit around the perimeter of the bottom of the tube. Place a tennis ball inside the container.

Horseshoes

Fill an empty half-liter soda bottle with pebbles to make a stake. Cut the center from plastic coffee can lids to make rings to serve as horseshoes.

Jingle Bell Blocks

Place jingle bells in empty square tissue boxes. Cover openings with duct tape or masking tape. Cover in colorful contact paper, if desired.

Kazoos

Give each child a piece of paper (4" x 6") to color. When they are finished help them glue the paper around an empty toilet paper tube. Secure a piece of wax paper over one end of the tube with a rubber band. Tape over the rubber band to keep it in place. Show the children how to make music with their kazoos.

Kite

Give children a paper bag. Invite them to color on the bag, making any designs they choose. When they are finished, place masking tape around the opening of the bag to reinforce it but don't tape it shut. Then, punch a hole through the tape on one side of the bag. Tie an 8' piece of yarn through the reinforced hole.

Leaf Preservation

Arrange several leaves between two 12" squares of clear contact paper.

Loud/Soft Shakers

Gather empty potato chip cans. Place heavy objects, such as pennies, washers, or pieces of gravel, in a few of the cans for a variety of loud sounds. Place lighter objects, such as paper clips, sand, and tabs from aluminum cans, in other shakers for softer sounds. Make sure lids are taped and/or glued securely

Magic Bottles

Gather three or four clear plastic bottles (empty 12-ounce soda bottles work well). Fill each bottle with a different liquid (cooking oil, white corn syrup, water, clear detergent). Then add a small object to each (marble, coin, small plastic toy, glitter or confetti). Make sure you glue and/or tape the tops on securely.

Magic Box

Cover a small box with brightly colored paper. Place several sizes of magnifying glasses in the box and perhaps a pair of binoculars. Place visually interesting items in the box and sit with children while they explore the items by looking at them through the magnifying glasses. Take a look outdoors with the binoculars. Point out the difference in the way things look when viewed through magnifying glasses and binoculars.

THE COMPLETE RESOURCE BOOK FOR INFANTS

Magic Wand

Make a magic wand using a cardboard tube from a coat hanger. Paint it and add a glittery star to the top.

Magnet Bottle

Fill a clean, empty half-liter bottle with broken-up Styrofoam packing pieces and several metal objects, such as paper clips, washers, buttons, pennies and so on. Glue and tape the lid on the bottle. Tie a magnet to one end of a piece of 12" piece of yarn and tie the other end of the yarn to the bottle.

Magnetic Photos

Ask family members to provide a picture or their baby. Photocopy, cut out, and laminate photos of the children. Glue a small magnetic strip to the back of each one.

Me Puzzles

Ask family members to provide a picture of their baby. Enlarge the copy the photos. Glue the photo on tag board or poster board. Laminate it and cut it into simple puzzle pieces.

Me and My Friend Photos

Ask family members to provide a picture of their baby. Enlarge photos of each baby and make a couple of photocopies of each. Glue each baby's picture onto one half of a piece of construction paper. Glue a friend's picture onto the other half. Cover with clear contact paper or laminate.

Mirror Hat

Use Velcro to attach a small, lightweight mirror to the front of an old hat (baseball caps work well).

Mystery Box

Cover a medium size box (copy paper boxes work well) and its lid in contact paper or fabric. Place question marks all over the box.

Observation Bottles

Fill clear, empty, half-liter soda bottles with a variety of interesting materials for the children to observe. Be sure to glue the lids on securely. Vary this according to the season, occasion, or the interests of the children. For example, adapt the bottles for seasonal observation by filling one bottle with seasonal items. A fall bottle might contain colored leaves and acorns.

Paper Bag Blocks

Use small paper bags. Fill each bag about half full with crumpled newspaper. Fold down the top and tape it closed.

Peek-a-Boo Photo

Glue a photocopied and enlarged picture of yourself to a paper plate. Play Peek-a-Boo using the Peek-a-Boo Photo to hide behind. Talk about what baby sees—first the real you, then your photo, and then the real you again.

Photo Box

Remove the lid of a copy paper box and cover the box with solid-color paper. Turn it upside down. Glue large, uncluttered, colorful photos on each side of the box. Use the box with infants during floor time.

who is it?

Photo Flappers

Use an X-acto knife to cut several flaps (peeping windows) in the left-hand side of a colored folder. Glue several small photos on the right hand side so that they line up with the flaps. Close the folder and glue or tape around the edges of the folder.

Plastic Bag Book

Stack 12 (based on the participation of 22 children) gallon-size, resealable plastic bags together. Staple them across the bottom to make the binding of the book. Cover the staples with a 2-inch-wide strip of colored vinyl tape. Make a cover for the book (you may want to list children's names on the back of the cover) and slip it into the first bag. Make a back cover to slip into the last bag. Slip children's artwork back-to-back into the other bags.

Potpourri Bottles

Fill an empty, clear one-liter plastic bottle with potpourri. Poke holes in the sides with a nail. Glue the lid on securely.

Pulley Bag

Cut a 6" x 12" piece of brightly colored felt. Fold the felt in half. Stitch two sides closed or use hot glue to close two sides. Fill the "bag" with cotton or wadded tissue paper. Then, close the last side of the bag. Punch a hole in one corner of the bag. Feed a plastic link through the hole. Add links to make a line 3' long. Attach the line loosely around the infant's ankle and throw the bag over the side of the crib. When the baby kicks, the bag will bounce up and down.

Sand Combs

Cut three or four pieces of poster board or cardboard into 3" x 6" strips. Cut teeth in one 6" side of each strip. Cut V-shaped (triangular) teeth in one and square teeth in another. Cutting scallops in another will give a circular look.

Scarf Pull

Tie or sew together ends/corners of three or four small scarves (try to use different colors and textures) to make one long scarf. Cut a slit in the lid of a potato chip can or oatmeal box. Stuff the scarf inside the can, pull an end through the lid, and then place the lid on the can. Make sure the lid is securely fastened with tape.

Sensory Glove

Fill a latex glove with Gak (see page 221) or with cornstarch or flour. Tie it off at the cuff.

Shape Sorting Box

Trace a few familiar objects that baby can hold (spoon, small block, toy car, ball, plastic cup, and so on) onto the bottom of a shoebox. Cut out their shapes with an Exacto knife. Let baby find the hole each object fits through.

Slot Drop Can

Cut a 1½" slot in the lid of an empty coffee can. Replace the lid. Provide poker chips or very large buttons for children to push through the Slot Drop Can. This is great practice for buttoning.

Slot Drop Variation

Cut two slits in the lid of a coffee can. Make one slit about ¼" wide and another about 1" wide. Make several fat chips by gluing four poker chips together. Single chips will work in the thin slit.

Sound Shakers

Use two small plastic containers (film canisters work great). Place several pennies in one for a heavy sound and a paper clip in another for a softer sound. **Safety Note**: Make sure lids are taped or glued on securely.

Spinning Face

Cut a 15" diameter circle out of cardboard or poster board. Draw a happy face on one side and a sad face on the other. Attach a piece of yarn to the face for suspending. Suspend the Spinning Face from the ceiling or from an empty wrapping paper tube bridging between two chairs.

Sticky Ball

Roll masking tape sticky side out into a ball.

Streamer Rings

Cut the center out of stiff paper plates or large coffee can lids. Tie or glue colored streamers around the outside.

Sunshine Puzzles

Cut circles from yellow construction paper. Draw happy faces on the circles. Laminate them and cut them into puzzle pieces.

Surprise Board

Enlarge a photo of yourself or use a large magazine photo. Glue the photo on a 12" x 12" piece of poster board. Cut a piece of fabric or use a scarf to tape over the face. Run the tape only across the top to create a flap. Use the board to play Peek-a-Boo with baby. Say, *peek,* and lift the flap.

 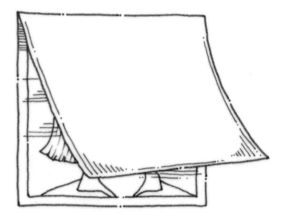

Tactile Blocks

Cover small and medium size cardboard boxes with fabrics that have a distinct texture, such as burlap, velvet, and satin.

Tactile Box

Cut a hole in the top or side of a shoebox. Fill the box with hard and soft items, such as small blocks, feathers, cotton balls, fabric scraps, and so on. Put the lid on the box and encourage little ones to reach inside and explore the size and texture of the items.

Texture Glove

Glue different textures of fabric to each finger of a work glove or a discarded regular glove. Use distinctly different feeling fabric, such as velvet, burlap, satin, and so on.

Texture Cards

Cut several 3" diameter cards from poster board. Cover the cards with fabrics of different textures, such as burlap, fur, net, and satin.

Textured Bottle Wraps

Cut 4" x 6" rectangles of textured fabric. Add a strip of Velcro fastener. Use these bottle covers to cover bottles during feeding time. Hold baby and encourage baby to hold the bottle. Talk about the feel of the fabric.

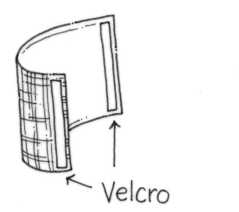

Velcro

Town Props

Draw trees and buildings on small white lunch sacks with markers. Stand props in the block center to create a town scene. Stabilize bags by placing a block inside of them.

Wave Machines

Collect several empty clear plastic bottles ranging in size from 20 ounces to one liter. Fill each bottle ¼ full with corn oil. Finish filling with denatured alcohol and a few drops of blue food coloring. Glue and tape lids on securely. If these spill, the mixture is very difficult to clean up.

Wind Catchers

Cut a paper plate in half. Cut colorful crepe paper streamers in 12" strips. Glue streamers on the curve of the half plates. Attach a string or piece of yarn to the flat edge of the plate and hang it outdoors on a breezy day.

"Getting to Know You" Survey

Child's Name: _____ Date: _____

Nickname: _____ (if applicable)

Family Member	Relationship
1)	
2)	
3)	
4)	
5)	

Ages of siblings: _____

What are your child's favorite toys? _____

_____

Has your child been separated from you before? Yes _____ No _____

If yes, please describe circumstances _____

_____

_____

Does your child exhibit any fears? Yes _____ No _____

If yes, please explain _____

_____

What do you hope your child will gain from his/her experience in group care?

_____

_____

_____

_____

Does your child have any allergies? Yes _____ No _____

If yes, please describe _____

_____

Page 2

Feeding Information

Preferences	Yes	No	Special Instructions
Warm Bottle			
Warm Food			
Feeds Self			
Uses Spoon			
Feeding Table			

Diapering Information

Condition	Ointment	Lotion	Powder	Special Instructions
Wet				
BM				
Rash				

Sleeping Preferences:

Position: Back _____ Side _____   Pacifier: Yes _____ No _____

Special Blanket: Yes _____ No _____   Special Toy: Yes _____ No _____

Current Sleeping Schedule: _____

_____

_____

_____

Is there anything else you would like us to know? _____

_____

_____

_____

_____

_____

Daily Report

Family Information for Caregiver

Child's name: _____ Arrival Time: _____ Date: _____

Sleeping Information: Slept Well _____   Slept Restlessly _____

Feeding Information: Bottle _____   Time: _____   Amount: _____

Breast _____   Time: _____   Amount: _____

Solids _____   Time: _____   Amount: _____

Special Instructions: _____

_____

_____

Caregiver Information to Family

Feeding Time	Food	Amount

Naps

From	To	Comments: _____
		_____
		_____

Bowel Movement: Yes _____   No _____   Normal _____   Loose _____

Something special your baby did today: _____

_____

_____

Baby Needs: Diapers ___   Wipes ___   Food ___   Juice ___   Cereal ___

Caregiver Signature: _____

Recommended Books for Infants

Books That Focus on Language Development

Animal Kisses by Barney Saltzberg

Apples and Pumpkins by Anne Rockwell

Baby Food by Margaret Miller

Baby Pets by Margaret Miller

Barnyard Banter by Denise Fleming

Brown Bear, Brown Bear, What Do You See? by Bill Martin, Jr.

The Foot Book by Dr. Seuss

Goodnight Moon by Margaret Wise Brown

Growing Vegetable Soup by Lois Ehlert

Hey! Little Baby by Nola Buck

Lunch by Denise Fleming

Moo, Baa, La La La! by Sandra Boynton

Mrs. Wishy Washy by Joy Cowley

Old MacDonald Had a Farm by Rosanne Litzinger

One Fish Two Fish Red Fish Blue Fish by Dr. Seuss

Opposites by Sandra Boynton

Pat the Bunny by Dorothy Kunhardt

The Pudgy Book of Mother Goose Rhymes by Richard Walz

The Wheels on the Bus by Todd South

Books That Focus on Social/Emotional Development

Baby Dance by Ann Taylor

The Baby Dances by Kathy Henderson

Baby Faces by Margaret Miller

Barnyard Dance! by Sandra Boynton

Bathtime, Colors, Playtime by Dorling Kindersley, Inc.

But Not the Hippopotamus by Sandra Boynton

Counting Kisses: A Kiss & Read Book by Karen Katz

Excuse Me!: A Little Book of Manners by Karen Katz

Five Little Monkeys Jumping on the Bed by Eileen Christelow

From Head to Toe by Eric Carle

Goodnight Moon by Margaret Wise Brown

Guess How Much I Love You by Sam McBratney

How a Baby Grows by Nola Buck

How Do I Feel? by Pamela Cote

Hug by Jez Alborough

I See Me! by Pegi Deitz Shea

Mr. Brown Can Moo, Can You? by Dr. Seuss

My Friends by Nancy Tafuri

No Biting! by Karen Katz

Pat the Bunny by Dorothy Kunhardt

Pretty Brown Face by Andrea and Brian Pinkney

Sheep in a Jeep by Nancy E. Shaw

Spot's Touch and Feel Day by Eric Hill

Tickle, Tickle by Helen Oxenbury

Toes, Ears, & Nose! by Marion Dane Bauer

Where Is Baby's Belly Button? by Karen Katz

Where Is Baby's Mommy? by Karen Katz

Books That Focus on Physical Development

Baby Dance by Ann Taylor

The Baby Dances by Kathy Henderson

Clap Hands by Helen Oxenbury

Clap Your Hands by Lorinda Bryan Cauley

From Head to Toe by Eric Carle

Hand, Hand, Fingers, Thumb by Al Perkin

Here Are My Hands by Bill Martin, Jr. and John Archambault

Piggies by Audrey Wood

Ten Little Fingers by Annie Kubler

Toddlerobics by Zita Newcome

Books That Focus on Cognitive Development

Baby Faces by Margaret Miller

Bounce Bounce Bounce by Kathy Henderson

Clap Hands by Helen Oxenbury

Do You Know New? by Jean Marzollo

Five Little Monkeys With Nothing to Do by Eileen Christelow

Five Little Monkeys Sitting in a Tree by Eileen Christelow

Hush Little Baby by Sylvia Long

I Love Colors by Margaret Miller

I Touch by Rachel Isadora

If You Give a Mouse a Cookie by Laura Joffe Numeroff

Itsy Bitsy Spider by Iza Trapani

Peek-a-Who? by Nina Laden

Red, Blue, Yellow Shoe by Tana Hoban

What Makes Me Happy? by Catherine and Laurence Anholt

What's on My Head? by Margaret Miller

Recommended CDs and Tapes

From Kimbo

Baby Faces

Baby Games

Diaper Gym

Dreamland

It's Toddler Time

Laugh 'n Learn Silly Songs

Nursery Rhyme Time

Singable Nursery Rhymes

Sweet Dreams

Toddlerific

From Thomas Moore Enterprises

Sleepy Time

From Melody House

Baby Can, Too

Rock the Baby by Mr. Al

From Wee Sing

Wee Sing for Babies by Pamela Beall and Susan Nipp

Wee Sing Nursery Rhymes and Lullabies by Pamela Beall and Susan Nipp

From Dayton Hudson

Songs to Dream By (Special collection from Marshall Fields)

Recommended Toys, Equipment, and Materials for Infants

Toys

- ☐ Bathtub toys
- ☐ Beanbags
- ☐ Busy boxes
- ☐ Crib toys
- ☐ Flashlights
- ☐ Floor puzzles
- ☐ Hats
- ☐ Jack-in-the-Box
- ☐ Jumbo magnetic letters
- ☐ Large magnets
- ☐ Large magnifying glass
- ☐ Large-piece puzzles
- ☐ Magnifying glasses
- ☐ Mobiles
- ☐ Musical toys
- ☐ Nesting toys
- ☐ Pattern blocks
- ☐ Plastic blocks

- ☐ Puppets
- ☐ Push toys and pull toys
- ☐ Rattles
- ☐ Rhythm band instruments
- ☐ Riding toys
- ☐ Rubber animals
- ☐ Sensory tubes
- ☐ Simple board books
- ☐ Snap beads
- ☐ Soft balls
- ☐ Sorting box
- ☐ Spinning tops and toys
- ☐ Squeeze toys and squeak toys
- ☐ Stacking rings
- ☐ Stuffed toys
- ☐ Toy telephones
- ☐ Unbreakable mirrors
- ☐ Wagons

Equipment

- ☐ Bottle warmer
- ☐ CD player
- ☐ CDs
- ☐ Changing table
- ☐ Crawling apparatus (soft pillows)
- ☐ Diaper container
- ☐ Feeding tables
- ☐ Flannel board
- ☐ Floor mats

- ☐ Individual cribs and bedding
- ☐ Infant seats
- ☐ Low shelving
- ☐ Low table with chairs
- ☐ Magnetic board
- ☐ Mobiles
- ☐ Refrigerator
- ☐ Rocker
- ☐ Small object tester

Materials (Consumables)

- ☐ Bottle warmer
- ☐ Bubble solution
- ☐ Butcher paper
- ☐ Chalk
- ☐ Construction paper
- ☐ Drawing paper
- ☐ Easel paint
- ☐ Fingerpaint

- ☐ Fingerpaint paper
- ☐ Glue
- ☐ Large crayons
- ☐ Markers
- ☐ Paste
- ☐ Playdough
- ☐ Tempera paint

Brain Basics

Senses

- Senses are ready for input right from birth and will continue to develop over the first few years of life. Research findings connect children's sensory experiences with brain activity and the development of the perceptual and behavioral competencies.
- Ninety-five percent of the information our brains process comes from our senses. Eighty-five percent comes from our vision, touch, and hearing.
- All early sounds, including music, influence the auditory wiring of the brain.
- An infant's hearing is wired well enough by the fifth month of gestation that he is able to hear sounds outside the womb.
- Wiring for vision is connected during the first two years of life. It is important for children to have many opportunities to refine their visual discrimination. Between the ages of two and five, vision wiring is enhanced through repetitive experiences examining visual images.
- The sense of taste is developed well enough to show preferences for sweets just days after birth. It continues to develop over the next few years. Introducing young children to a variety of foods helps refine their sense of taste.
- An interesting finding related to hearing is that babies can remember patterns of sounds, such as the rhythm or cadence of a story read over and over, or the melody and words of a song. Infants will frequently turn their heads toward the source of a familiar sound.

Memory

- The use of small muscles enhances memory. Hands-on activities are helpful to children when they are learning new skills.
- Emotions boost memory. The endorphins that are released with emotional responses act as a memory fixative.

Repetition

- Repetition of skills is critical to mastery. When children practice what they have learned by repeating an activity, they expand their understanding of that skill. Think about riding a bicycle. Every time you ride you become better at balancing. New experiences provide expanded knowledge. Your muscles become stronger from repeated use. Your awareness of bicycle etiquette expands. And, most important, your self-confidence increases, allowing you to try more difficult tasks.
- Repetition is critical to the storing of information in long-term memory. What we repeat once in 30 days we have only a 10% chance of remembering. What we repeat six times in 30 days we have a 90% chance of remembering.

■ Rereading familiar stories coincides with the way children learn. The repetition improves their vocabulary, sequencing, and memory skills. Research shows that children often ask as many, and sometimes the same questions, after a dozen readings as they do after the first reading. This is because they are learning language in increments—not all at once. Each reading brings a little more meaning to the story. Children love to hear a story over and over again.

Water and Nutrition

■ The brain is 85% water. It needs water to operate.

■ Thirsty brains can't think. The brain needs water to stay alert; water fuels our neurotransmitters (the chemicals that carry information from one neurological community to another neurological community). Water should be consumed throughout the day and in proportion to both body size and activity.

■ Water increases metabolism by 3%.

■ Infants can become over hydrated. Their kidneys are not fully functional until around the fourth month. They should be introduced to water by doctor's directions.

■ Brain foods include proteins, such as seeds, lentils, milk, cheese, eggs, meat and fish, whole grains, such as rye, millet, brown rice, oats, and wheat, and flax. Flax provides fat that coats nerve fibers that help the brain work more efficiently. Nuts are also a good brain food but present choking and allergy hazards for infants.

■ Children use 48% of their calorie intake to fuel their brain. Adults use 20%. A child's brain is 2½ times more active than an adult's brain.

Oxygen

■ Oxygen fuels the chemicals in the brain, the neurotransmitters. It helps keep the brain alert.

■ The brain requires 20% of the oxygen in the body to function alertly.

■ Studies suggest that only 32% of the population has enough oxygen in their bodies to effectively fuel the brain.

■ Exercise helps increase body oxygen.

■ Plants in the classroom increase the oxygen in the room.

Choice

■ Choices allow learners to match personal goals with instructional goals. They increase the motivation to learn.

■ Choices for very young children (birth to three) should be limited to two options. For older children (three to six) choices should be limited to three. Making good choices requires that the brain coordinate multiple input systems. Too many choices cause the brain to shut down from over stimulation.

Novelty

- The brain loves novelty. It will pay closer attention to new information and new environmental stimulus.
- Rotating toys and wall decorations increases the probability that infants will attend to the toy and information on the wall.

Patterns

- The brain is constantly searching for patterns. It organizes information by assessing patterns. Learning takes place as the brain examines new information and assesses how the information is like what it already knows and how the information is different from what it already knows. When the brain accommodates the differences, learning takes place.
- Intelligence is the ability to see patterns and build relationships out of those patterns.

Problem Solving

- The brain "feeds" on problem solving. It is constantly searching for solutions.
- Self-esteem is directly related to one's ability to solve problems.

Colors

- Reds, yellows, and oranges increase brain alertness. Blues, purples, and greens have a calming effect on the brain.
- Pale yellow, in moderation, is the optimum color for learning.
- Red increases appetite. Blue represses appetite.

Aromas

- Peppermint, basil, and cinnamon increase mental alertness.
- Lavender, rose, and orange calm the brain.

American Sign Language Signs

Baby

Brother

Chin

Daddy

Down

Ears

Eyes

Finger

Finished

Goodbye

Hair

Hands

Hello

Hug

I Love You

Me

THE COMPLETE RESOURCE BOOK FOR INFANTS

Mommy

More

Mouth

No

Nose

Please

Sister

Stop

Thank You

Yes

Developmental Checklist

Age	Skills	Date
Birth to 4 months	Displays sensory awareness--see, hear, taste, smell, feel	
	Develops distance vision-- at birth--9" to 14"; at 1 month--1' to 2'; at 3 months--6'to 8'	
	Cries to express needs	
	Enjoys social interactions	
	Begins to turn head	
	Makes eye contact	
	Makes cooing sounds	
	Smiles	
	Lifts head to look around	
	Turns head toward a familiar voice	
	Grasps a small object	
	Tracks an object moving from side to side	
3 months to 7 months	Reaches for objects	
	Expresses happiness and sadness	
	Supports upper body with arms when on stomach	
	Looks at hands and feet	
	Bats or hits at an object	
	Enjoys looking in a mirror	
	Rolls over	
	Recognizes familiar people	
	Plays "Peek-a-Boo"	
	Begins to show understanding of cause and effect	
	Attempts to pull up	
	Bounces when standing on an adult's lap	
	Holds a bottle	
6 months to 10 months	Sits unassisted	
	Looks for an items when dropped	
	Looks for an item when hidden under a pillow	
	Drops things on purpose	
	Changes an object from one hand to the other	
	Rocks on hands and knees	
	Mimics actions	
	Mimics sounds	
	Babbles a string of sounds	

THE COMPLETE RESOURCE BOOK FOR INFANTS

Age	Skills	Date
6 months to 10 months (continued)	Pulls up to a standing position	
	Makes purposeful noise	
	Puts small items in mouth	
	Feeds self finger foods	
	Looks at pictures when named	
	Picks things up	
	Pushes and shoves things	
9 months to 13 months	Crawls	
	Recognizes familiar words	
	Takes off clothing	
	Fits nesting boxes together	
	Waves goodbye	
	Crawls, scoots, creeps	
	Follows simple directions	
	Looks at a book	
	Remembers where familiar items are kept	
	Drops thing into an open box	
	Scoops items	
	Begins to roll a ball	
	Babbles, mimicking speech	
	Tears paper	
	Copies simple gestures	
	Scribbles	
12 months to 19 months	Approximates simple words	
	Moves around the room	
	Plays simple pretend games	
	Puts items in and takes them out of a container	
	Uses one-word sentences	
	Plays simple musical instruments	
	Hands items to someone	
	Helps dress and undress self	
	Rolls a ball	
	Uses identification words correctly	
	Enjoys looking at a book	
	Retrieves ball that has rolled out of sight	
	Walks upstairs with help	
	Notes differences in temperature, smell, and taste	
	Attempts to sing a song	

Age	Skills	Date
12 months to 19 months (continued)	Enjoys messy play	
	Points at familiar objects	
	Hugs and kisses	
	Recognizes self in mirror	
	Stacks two or more blocks	
	Turns two or three pages of a book at a time	
	Tries to kick a ball	
	Shows one or more body parts	
	Pushes, pulls, or carries a toy while walking	
	Places pegs in holes	
	Uses a spoon to scoop	
18 months to 24 months	Throws a ball	
	Attempts walking up and down stairs	
	Shows a variety of emotions	
	Chews food	
	Zips and unzips	
	Points to several body parts	
	Walks on wide balance board	
	Rides a small riding toy	
	Enjoys nursery rhymes and songs	
	Says two-word sentences	
	Unwraps packages with a little starter help	
	Matches sounds to animals	
	Turns book pages one at a time	
	Enjoys water play	
	Sings word of a song (at least some)	
	Attempts to jump in place	
	Repeats words you say	
	Works a simple puzzle	
	Strings large beads	
	Uses playdough	
	Uses finger paint	
	Holds pictures right side up	
	Uses words that tell what an object does	
	Recognizes self in a picture	
	Runs	
	Listens to a short story	
	Tries to balance on one foot	

Resources for Caregivers

Books

Bailey, B. 2000. *I Love You Rituals*. New York: HarperCollins.

Ramey, C. & S. Ramey. 1999. *Right From Birth*. New York: Goddard Press, Inc.

Schiller, P. 1999. *Start Smart: Building Brain Power in the Early Years*. Beltsville, MD: Gryphon House.

Silberg, J. 1993. *Games to Play With Babies*. Beltsville, MD: Gryphon House.

Silberg, J. 2000. *125 Brain Games for Babies*. Beltsville, MD: Gryphon House.

Websites

http://www.kidshealth.com

http://www.iamyourchild.org

http://www.naeyc.org

http://www.zerotothree.org

http://www.seca.org

http://www.familyeducation.com/home

References

Baker, A. & L. Manfredi-Pettit. 2004. ***Relationships, the heart of quality care***. Washington, DC: National Association for the Education of Young Children.

Brazelton, T. B. 1992. ***Touchpoints: Your child's emotional and behavioral development***. Reading, MA: Perseus Publishing.

Bredekamp, S. & C. Copple. 1997. ***Developmentally appropriate practice in the early childhood classroom, revised edition***. Washington, DC: National Association for the Education of Young Children.

Gopnik, A., A. Meltzoff, & P. Kuhl. 2001. ***The scientist in the crib: What early learning tells us about the mind***. New York: Perennial Currents.

Huttenlocher, J, et al. 1991. Early vocabulary growth: Relation to language input and gender. ***Developmental Psychology***, 27: 236-248.

Jensen, E. 1995. ***The learning brain***. Del Mar, CA: Turning Point.

Kotulak, R. April 11, 1993. "Unraveling hidden mysteries of the brain." ***Chicago Tribune***, p. 11.

Nash, M. 1997. "Fertile minds." ***Time Magazine***, 149, no. 5: 48-56.

Ramey, C. & S. Ramey. 1999. ***Right from birth: Building your child's foundation for life***. New York: Goddard Press.

Schiller, P. (1999). *Start Smart: Building Brain Power in the Early Years*. Beltsville, MD: Gryphon House.

Shore, R. 1997. *Rethinking the brain: New insights into early development*. New York: Families and Work Institute.

THE COMPLETE RESOURCE BOOK FOR INFANTS

Children's Book Index

Index